To Phil

kindfulness

be a true friend to yourself —
with mindful self-compassion

padraig o'morain

First published in Great Britain in 2018 by Yellow Kite
An imprint of Hodder & Stoughton
An Hachette UK company

This paperback edition published in 2019

1

To preserve confidentiality, the examples in this book disguise the identities of
persons concerned through the changing of details, the transposition of situations
and the use of composite characters. In that sense, the characters are fictional
though their dilemmas are real.

A CIP catalogue record for this title is available from the British Library

Paperback ISBN 978 1 473 67878 1

Typeset in Bembo Std by Palimpsest Book Production Limited, Falkirk, Stirlingshire

Printed and bound in Great Britain by Clays Ltd, Elcograf S.p.A.

Hodder & Stoughton policy is to use papers that are natural,
renewable and recyclable products and made from wood grown in sustainable
forests. The logging and manufacturing processes are expected to conform
to the environmental regulations of the country of origin.

Yellow Kite
Hodder & Stoughton Ltd
Carmelite House
50 Victoria Embankment
London EC4Y 0DZ

www.yellowkitebooks.co.uk
www.hodder.co.uk

CONTENTS

ACKNOWLEDGEMENTS

Those who have taken part in my courses over the years – offline and online – have enriched my understanding of mindfulness and self-compassion more than I have enriched theirs.

My family tolerated, with good humour, my disappearance into the process of writing this book.

Dr Kristin Neff, whose work I refer to in the text; along with that of other figures in various disciplines, has made a great contribution to our understanding of mindfulness, especially through her research.

Finally, my publisher, Liz Gough, my editor, Julia Kellaway and my agent, Susan Feldstein, must take the credit for ushering this book onto the shelves.

'Today I befriend
the person I
already am.'

1

SELF-COMPASSION: STARTING THE JOURNEY

Kate has always felt she could be a better person. She could be successful, confident, generous and popular.

Her friends would say she already has a reasonable degree of success, confidence, generosity and popularity, but Kate doesn't really see it that way.

That nagging feeling that if people could see what she was really like they would know she was not good enough stays with her through her days and nights. It's like a permanent shadow: she doesn't always notice it, but it's always there.

Kate searches books and articles for ideas on how to make her into a person she can like and approve of. She has spent many free hours on the Internet in this search.

Over the years, many books and articles have promised to help her to become that person. Each time, she has set about their suggested self-improvement projects with hope.

Sadly, she has never found the right one. Still, she goes on searching.

Is this the book she's been looking for?

No, it isn't.

WHAT THIS BOOK IS AND WHAT IT ISN'T

This is a book which aims to help you – and Kate – to practise self-compassion. This means that it isn't about self-*improvement*. You mightn't be a better person by the time you finish this book because, as we journey through it together, we're going to side-step the whole self-improvement thing.

That isn't to say that self-improvement is a bad thing. By and large it's a good thing; it only turns bad when it never ends, when you never learn to like the person you already are, when you become like a person who gets addicted to cosmetic surgery but who never likes who they see in the mirror.

This book will help you to like the person who has come this far on the journey with you, the one who is reading this book right now. It will help you to like the person in the mirror, flaws and all.

Kate could tell you she lives with someone unsatisfactory whom she would like to get away from. She can't get away from that person, though, because that person is Kate.

Pushing yourself out of the door is, I would imagine, impossible. Getting to like the person you already are is a far more workable alternative. Why don't more of us choose that alternative more of the time? Surely it's easier than endlessly postponing the day we can really like, and fully approve of, ourselves? I will say more on this later when I mention Sigmund Freud and other great psychologists of the past century (page 5).

SELF-COMPASSION IS AN INSIDE JOB

This book also isn't about self-esteem. We will side-step that too. Self-esteem so often relies on external factors, such as other people's approval or events that make you feel like a winner, but which may have been outside of your control. For instance, if you're in Sales you get a kick, I hope, out of making a sale. It feels really good to know you were able to increase the chances, using your skills and experience, of a customer buying your product. However, the ultimate control lies with the customer and not with you. Still, if this – a successful sale – happens many times in a row, your self-esteem will get a boost: you'll feel like a winner. But if you fail to sell many times in a row, and if you have based your self-esteem on your prowess as a salesperson, then your self-esteem will fall: you'll feel like a loser.

Self-compassion doesn't depend on external forces. You don't need an applauding audience to experience it. You can give compassion to yourself even if you have 'low self-esteem' or even if you fail to make those sales.

That's the truly good news for Kate. She can drop the search for that 'perfect' person by giving the gift of compassion to her imperfect self.

A FRIEND TO WHO YOU ARE

So your starting point – and also your finishing point – is to be a friend to the person you already are, with all your virtues, faults and foibles.

In my work as a counsellor over the years I have learned how very damaging it can be for people to dislike themselves. As I have said, it's like a permanent shadow and, as you read through this book, I think you will come to see how thoroughly it influences your one and only life.

In a sense, wanting to change yourself is a hallmark of our global culture, so if you think you need improvement, you are not alone. All over the world, lots of people take to the gym or to pounding the streets in January. If they are just doing this because they want to be fit and healthy, that's one thing. But if they're doing it to win their own approval, in the hope that they might finally be able to start liking themselves at the end, they're getting it the wrong way round; the message of this book is: like yourself first.

If they can manage that, they will have gained what might be described as 'psychological liberation'. Then they can go running if they want to.

When you have to work hard to get your own approval, you are shackled by that need. Think of how much you do or put up with so that you will become a person you can like. But suppose you could like the person you already are. Wouldn't that be liberation and wouldn't it free up your life choices? This doesn't mean you'll never work hard again,

4

but you'll have a different reason, perhaps the satisfaction of a job well done for instance.

EVERYONE'S A CRITIC

Why do we criticise ourselves so much? Why is a book like this even necessary? Self-criticism seems to be built into us to an unhelpful degree. Many of our most important psychological writers have noted this:

- According to Sigmund Freud, the often controversial but still towering figure in psychoanalysis, each of us has a part of the mind that is relentlessly critical. He called it the 'superego'. It can make you feel bad about anything: your choice of career, your choice of partner, your failure to choose a partner, that big slice of Black Forest gateau you've just eaten, those silly socks you're wearing, that wicked thought you've just had – it has a wide and varied menu of issues to complain about.

- Albert Ellis, who developed 'Rational Emotive Behaviour Therapy', listed the many irrational beliefs that make life more difficult for us. Of these, one of the most common is the idea that 'I must impress all the people who are important to me and, if I don't, it will be terrible'. This idea is irrational because we can't impress everybody all the time. And many of those who are important to us would rather feel connected to us than impressed by us.

Ellis restated that irrational demand along those lines: 'It would be great to impress all the people who are important to me, but that's impossible and it's by no means terrible that I can't.'

- Carl Rogers, who could be described as the father of counselling, said we set conditions which we must meet before we regard ourselves as worthwhile. He called these 'conditions of worth'. Very often, these conditions are set so high we can't meet them, so we can very easily go through life seeing ourselves as not good enough. In this book, I describe those conditions as 'sacred cows' and self-compassion can help you to critically assess your sacred cows and only keep the helpful ones (see Chapter 7 for more on this).

Here is a key takeaway point from these theorists:

Even if you become the 'perfect' person you think you ought to be, you will still criticise yourself. You cannot impress the critic in your head so much that he or she shuts up. That's why you need self-compassion.

HOW SELF-COMPASSION CAN FREE US

With self-compassion:

- You practise accepting the person you already are without

making yourself jump through rings of fire to become 'acceptable' to your internal critic.

- Your aim is to take a friendly attitude towards yourself and to know that you have your own friendship, no matter what.

- If you need to make changes in your behaviour, you will do so from a standpoint of friendship towards yourself and not of hostility.

This is our starting point: adopting an attitude of friendship towards yourself with all of the faults that you have right now, and knowing that, even if you fall flat on your face, you will still be that friend.

Will this turn you into a selfish monster? No, it won't. Research shows that self-compassionate people are more likely to behave well towards others. What's more, liking yourself won't rob you of all ambition; people who are self-compassionate are actually more willing to take a chance. Why? Because they know they won't attack themselves mercilessly if they fail.

HOW MINDFULNESS HELPS

- Mindfulness practice improves our capacity for compassion. This has been established in studies by neuroscientists. What this book will help you to do is to turn some of that compassion towards yourself. Moreover, you will learn many simple mindfulness practices throughout the book - adopt the few that appeal to you most and make them a regular part of your life.

- Mindfulness also enables us to spot when we are not being self-compassionate. Awareness - a core aspect of mindfulness - enables us to spot harmful patterns of thinking and to do something about them. Our awareness improves as we practise mindfulness using the easy methods you will learn about throughout this book.

Mindfulness and self-compassion work in harmony – coming together as 'kindfulness' – and I hope you will experience this pleasant development in yourself as you continue to read this book.

Throughout the book you will find practices and affirmations. Both will help you to get the most out, of the 'lessons' I outline in each chapter. If you try them out, you will learn what your favourite practices and affirmations are, and you can make them part of your cultivation of self-compassion.

Many of the practices are aimed specifically at helping you to develop mindfulness. Others are aimed specifically at helping you to cultivate self-compassion. Add mindfulness to self-compassion and you have that powerful combination called kindfulness.

Affirmations are simply thoughts that you introduce to your mind because they are helpful and because they can change the tone of your thinking from negative to positive. They are not mystical or magical, but they are well worth using because thoughts are so important to how we experience the world and to how we face challenges.

SO WHAT IS 'KINDFULNESS'?

The three components of kindfulness – mindful self-compassion – are woven into what you have read so far. I have adapted them from the description of self-compassion by Dr Kristin Neff, who is an internationally recognised researcher on the subject. They are:

1. To extend friendship to the person you already are.

2. To be mindful so that you can spot the destructive patterns of thinking that lead you to treat yourself like an enemy and so that you can open a space for self-compassion.

3. To remember our common humanity, specifically that we share our faults and virtues with millions of others.

You'll read much more on all of these in the book but first let's try some self-compassion and mindfulness practices.

Self-compassion and Mindfulness Practices

Try out these practices over the next few days:

MINDFUL BREATH

At least three times a day pause for a minute or so and notice the sensation of your breath at the entrance to your nostrils.

You don't have to push your breath or do anything special with it. Simply notice it.

When your mind wanders, as it will, during this simple task, silently say the word 'thinking' and return your attention to your breath. Do so with compassion and without self-criticism. Minds wander. That is what they do. Simply bring your attention back when you discover that it has gone away.

The purpose of this exercise is to help you to develop your general capacity for mindfulness.

YOU ARE NOT ALONE

Next time you spot yourself having self-critical thoughts, pause for a moment to become aware of the many hundreds and thousands, or perhaps millions, of people who are having a thought similar to yours:

'Why didn't I do something different with my life?'
'I shouldn't have eaten that Italian ice cream last night.'
  'I wish I hadn't said that thing I said that was foolish and hurtful.'

You are not the only person having these thoughts or a thought that is very similar. Realising that you are not unique in these experiences is a necessary step towards self-compassion.

AFFIRMATION

'Today I befriend the person I already am.'

If you put conditions on your own friendship towards yourself, then what happens if you cannot meet those conditions?

Should a parent deny a child friendship because he or she is not perfect? Of course not. We know that the denial of friendship under such circumstances introduces an element of unnecessary and unhelpful pain into a child's emotional life. So why do this to yourself?

Why not use this affirmation first thing in the morning? It's a far better way to start the day than grumbling about yourself or about whatever you've got to do before you get back to your bed tonight!

REMEMBER THIS . . .

The person towards whom you need to be self-compassionate is the person you are right now.

If you wait until you achieve perfection, you may be waiting for a long time! In any case, the perfect person doesn't need your compassion – it's the imperfect person you are right now who needs it.

Self-compassion isn't about becoming a better person and liking that person – it's about liking who you are.

NOTES

- **Albert Ellis** developed Rational Emotive Behaviour Therapy. An often controversial figure, he is seen by many as having brought about the development of cognitive behavioural therapy. He believed we live by irrational rules, such as 'I must be a high achiever or else I am worthless' and his therapy includes identifying and disputing these rules. More: www.albertellis.org

- **Sigmund Freud**, the great and controversial psychoanalyst, saw the human psyche as comprising the moralistic and often harsh 'superego', the 'id', which seeks immediate gratification and isn't concerned with morality, and the 'ego', which tries to balance out the conflict between the superego and the id. We usually identify with the ego. More: www.simplypsychology.org/psyche.html

- **Dr Kristin Neff** teaches, researches and writes on self-compassion. She is an associate professor at the department of Educational Psychology, University of Texas at Austin. She is the author of *Self-Compassion: Stop*

Beating Yourself Up and Leave Insecurity Behind and is a leading figure in bringing the practice of self-compassion to a wider audience. More: www.self-compassion.org

'Twenty thousand breaths. This one compassionate.'

2

ADD A LITTLE
MINDFULNESS

George likes to get on with things. Beating about the bush is something he has no time whatsoever for. He only came to a mindfulness and self-compassion workshop because his employer had included it in a 'wellness week' for staff. He could see the value of self-compassion but was quite dismissive of the idea of making the practice of mindfulness a key part of that process.

'What is the point', he asked, 'of sitting there concentrating on my breathing if what I really want to do is to feel better about myself? There's no connection at all between the two.'

I pointed out to George that research shows a very clear connection between mindfulness and self-compassion. Mindfulness stimulates greater activity in the insula, a part of the brain that plays a key role in developing empathy. Empathy leads to compassion and we can direct some of that compassion towards ourselves if we so choose.

MINDFULNESS: NOT JUST SITTING AROUND

'But isn't mindfulness just sitting there in the lotus posture staring ahead doing nothing for hours?' No, it's not, though this may very well be the media's favourite image of mindfulness – beautiful people in perfect yoga postures watching the sun rise or even besuited executives squatting on a desk, meditating. This is ridiculous and has nothing whatsoever to do with the real thing.

The vast majority of people who have practised mindfulness throughout history have never sat in the lotus posture or meditated for hours – among other things, they were too busy putting food on the table. Anyway, most of us would find the lotus posture a very painful position after a while!

Cultivating mindfulness can make all the difference to self-compassion, as George would find out.

TAKE HALF A STEP BACK

George agreed that he tended to judge other people and himself very quickly. Well, if he was a man who rushed to judgement, I suggested, maybe he could accept that he was now doing exactly that with regards to mindfulness.

In practising mindfulness, he would learn to 'take half a step back' (to borrow a concept from Zen Buddhism) instead of rushing into some highly critical judgement of himself or somebody else.

That 'half a step back' would also make it easier for him to spot when he's not being compassionate towards himself. That awareness, in itself, would be a major help to him in changing how he sees himself.

As we worked on mindfulness, I found that George gradually became less critical and less quick to rush to judgement, and I began to see a softer side of him. He hadn't yet begun to see that side of himself because he hadn't yet begun to direct compassion in his own direction.

FROM MINDFULNESS TO COMPASSION

Gradually, and with some scepticism, George began to think of himself as deserving at least some of his own compassion and soon he reported that his feelings about himself had begun to change in a very positive direction. In fact, he soon became a very enthusiastic practitioner of mindfulness.

But what is mindfulness and why do it?

- As a practice, mindfulness means returning your attention from your wandering mind to what's happening in the moment.
- By returning your attention with compassion for yourself you cultivate kindness towards yourself, and therefore kindfulness (mindful self-compassion).

- Why would mindfulness lead to self-compassion? Because, as I mentioned at the start of this chapter, mindfulness increases empathy – a sense of what other people are feeling – because of its effect on the brain. And empathy is a component of compassion, perhaps even the very heart of it.

MINDFULNESS AND ACCEPTANCE

Let's look at this in a little more detail, especially with regards to acceptance, which is a crucial element of mindfulness.

As I said above, mindfulness is returning your attention again and again to whatever is going on in the moment.

- What do you return your attention from? From the thoughts that can so easily get you caught up in their stories and from the self-criticisms that can so easily accompany these stories. The mind is continually gener-ating thoughts and we tend to follow those thoughts and get lost in them. This is so even though they are usually thoughts we have had many times before and even though we often gain nothing from letting them take us away from our awareness of the present moment.
- What do you return your attention to? To your breathing, your walking, washing the dishes, driving . . . whatever is actually going on in the moment. That sounds simple, but because we naturally wander off in our heads, mindfulness needs constant practice. Moreover, the present moment isn't always fun and exciting: washing the dishes or standing in the queue for the bus is rarely a laugh a

minute. But this simple practice is what brings us the benefits of mindfulness. Even a dull moment is your moment and is part of your life.

When you bring your attention back in mindfulness practice, you do so with acceptance of your experience. Acceptance is a core aspect of mindfulness and we will return to it in more detail in Chapter 3 (page 27).

ACCEPTANCE AND CHANGE

Will acceptance make you lazy about change? No, acceptance doesn't mean that you will never change anything about yourself. It enables you to create a sort of quiet space in your mind in which you can be aware of what's going on for you. Think of this as 'simply knowing' without getting lost in scolding yourself or – depending on what's happening – in feeling sorry for yourself. Scolding and feeling sorry for yourself can divert your energy and attention from what you need to do. On the other hand, an attitude of self-acceptance with understanding, with curiosity and without attacking yourself enables you to look in a self-compassionate way at changes you need to make.

Suppose you have an exam coming up in a month and you've been putting off preparing for it because you're nervous about the fact that you haven't been preparing for it. The non-mindful, non-accepting way to deal with this would be to keep putting off thinking about it until a tomorrow that never comes. Finally, when the stress gets too great, you revise late into the night, feeling miserable about the exam and about yourself.

In mindful acceptance you can say that, yes, you are nervous and, yes, you haven't been doing enough work on it and, yes, you need to start revising now and not in three weeks' time. You do all this without criticism of yourself and you can then set up a far easier programme of study than if you had put it all off for three weeks.

A more common, everyday example would be forgetting to set the alarm and waking up late for work. What's to be gained from launching into a series of attacks on yourself? Nothing.

Instead what you need to do is to remember to set the alarm tonight, and that's it. You're probably going to do a little self-criticising almost by reflex, but what's important is to be able to come out of that reaction rather quickly and to get on with things. The more you practise mind-fulness the easier you will find acceptance.

So first of all, mindfulness gives you that space, that pause, in which to step back from what's going on in your head and your emotions. And because we can so quickly get lost in our reactions and our self-criticisms, that pause is really important – it enables us to step out of the river of thoughts carrying us away and instead to stand on the bank, observe what's going on and make calm choices.

MINDFULNESS CULTIVATES
SELF-COMPASSION

As I've explained, the practice of mindfulness cultivates our sense of compassion for others because it increases our sense of empathy. Empathy is an appreciation of how other people might be feeling and it is a necessary component of compassion.

Now, it is entirely possible to be very compassionate towards other people and uncompassionate towards yourself (this has been demonstrated in research by Dr Kristin Neff of the University of Texas at Austin) and that's why we need to remember to turn some of that compassion in our own direction.

Again, mindfulness helps with this. How? By enabling us to remember that we ourselves are deserving of some of our own compassion.

According to Professor Mark Williams, the original meaning of the word 'mindfulness' ('*satipatthana*' in the Pāli language in which many of the old Buddhist texts were written down) is 'to remember', in the sense of remembering where you are, what you are or what you are doing.

So, if you're lost in the practice of giving yourself a hard time in your head, mindfulness can help you to remember your intention to be self-compassionate instead of continuing on and on barking at yourself.

'THINKING' – BRINGING YOURSELF BACK

In the mindful breathing practice in the first chapter (page 10), I asked you to silently say the word 'thinking' to yourself whenever you discover that your mind has wandered off into its usual stories about the past, the present, the future, the shopping list, your life, etc. I also asked you to do that in a self-compassionate way. So when you get to the mindfulness practices part of this chapter (page 23) I want you to really focus on that self-compassionate way of saying the word 'thinking' and bringing yourself back.

In bringing yourself back, it is all too easy to say to yourself, 'Oh, here I go again – my stupid mind has wandered off, how disappointing'. That's not the way to do it. The way to do it is to notice with compassion and kindness that you are thinking. Then, the word 'thinking' becomes a simple way to bring yourself into mindfulness with self-compassion – into kindfulness.

The Buddhist teacher Pema Chödrön points out that when we say 'thinking' in that compassionate way, it trains us in developing gentleness towards ourselves. By the way, 'thinking' is not the only word you could use. I also like to use phrases such as 'not happening now' or 'come back' – the aim is to break the chain of rumination so you can use whatever word you like.

I will also ask you in the practices section, to do a very simple 'body scan'. To do this, I want you to bring awareness to the top of your head and then move it all the way down, in stages, to your feet. What's really important here is that you encounter each part of your body with compassion. Even if it is a part of your body that you think has let you down, that you are ashamed of or that you scold, I want you to relate to it with compassion while doing the body scan.

Remember, the key is to be mindful in a self-compassionate way – show your body kindfulness.

Self-compassion and Mindfulness Practices

MINDFULNESS OF BREATHING WITH COMPASSION

Now and then, take a minute or two to bring your awareness to your breathing. You can do this in any way you prefer – my own preference is to notice my breath at the entrance to my nostrils. As you try to be aware of your breathing, you will find that your mind will drift many times. Every time you realise this has happened, say the word 'thinking' and bring your attention back.

Say 'thinking' with compassion towards yourself and without in any way criticising yourself for your mind-wandering.

A BODY SCAN WITH COMPASSION

Bring awareness to the top of your head. Now move your awareness down along your head to your shoulders, down your chest and tummy and back, arms and hands, your hips, your thighs, knees, calves and feet.

As you do this, try to generate a sense of compassion towards your body. If you encounter tension or pain in your body, or if you encounter parts of your body that you are not happy with, do so with compassion. Approach them, at least during the body scan, with a sense of kindness towards yourself and towards each part of your body.

If you find it difficult to generate a feeling of kindness, do the body scan with the intention of being kind to your body. Gradually, the feeling will follow the intention.

AFFIRMATION

'Twenty thousand breaths. This one compassionate.'

We take at least 20,000 breaths a day, usually outside our awareness. Every one of those breaths is taken in the present moment, so bringing attention to our breathing brings us into the here and now. Adding a sense of compassion to the breath brings self-compassion to the moment.

REMEMBER THIS . . .

Come back to the moment with compassion for the one who's coming back. It is you as you are now who needs compassion. Deliberately giving yourself compassion as you return deliberately to this moment is a great way to cultivate this invaluable practice.

NOTES

- **Professor Mark Williams** is a leading authority in mindfulness research. His findings that mindfulness practice can help people with recurring depression to greatly cut the rate of relapse have been very influential. For instance, the UK's National Health Service includes mindfulness as a recommended treatment for people who have been depressed three times or more. His books include *Mindfulness: A Practical Guide to Finding Peace in a Frantic World* (with Dr Danny Penman). More: YouTube has many excellent talks by Professor Williams.

- **Pema Chödrön** is an American Buddhist nun (in the Tibetan tradition) and writer. Her books include *When Things Fall Apart* and *Start Where You Are*. More: www.pemachodronfoundation.org

'I accept this reality.'

3

ACCEPTANCE: THE OTHER HALF OF MINDFULNESS

Some people hide from themselves. Marilyn was one of these people. She didn't like to look at herself in the mirror and she didn't particularly like thinking about herself. Marilyn had come from a long line of people whose favourite word was 'unacceptable'. In fact, her family had a reputation for awkwardness or 'contrariness', stretching back at least two generations, in the village from which she came.

Marilyn brought this approach into her adult life. Her habit of seeing all faults – small and large – as unacceptable had already wrecked her marriage and was in danger of wrecking her relationship with her two children.

At work, Marilyn was an efficient and effective team leader, except that the members of her team tended to move on as soon as they could. Her attitude that the slightest lapse from how she wanted things done was unacceptable drove them away. One member of her team had even accused Marilyn of bullying because she had continuously described their work as unacceptable and this was ultimately what had led to Marilyn coming to a course recommended by a colleague.

But Marilyn also found many aspects of herself unacceptable. She always saw herself as falling short in any project she undertook at work, despite her reputation as somebody who could be depended upon to get anything done and done well. Unfortunately, she had acquired the idea that if anything you do is unacceptable, then you are unacceptable. That's why Marilyn does not like looking in mirrors. She feels she is looking at an unacceptable person.

Firstly, I encouraged Marilyn to learn to accept minor differences in others and then her own minor faults. I then encouraged Marilyn to learn to accept herself. Over time I could see her blossoming. I could see the tension falling away as she discovered the huge benefits of acceptance. That process was helped by her realisation that acceptance and self-compassion do not lead to a lowering of standards or to reckless behaviour.

Acceptance

Acceptance can be a powerful force in our lives. It is an essential aspect of mindfulness and self-compassion, and is therefore interlinked with the concept of kindfulness. Strangely, while most people know that mindfulness requires returning your awareness more often to the present moment, many have never heard of the value of acceptance in mindfulness. I often say that acceptance is the other half of mindfulness and that it may be the better half.

In fact, mindfulness without acceptance is not really mindfulness at all and the same can be said of self-compassion. We often hear mindfulness described as awareness, but it's more than that: it's awareness with acceptance. For instance, you might be aware that you feel anxious but it's when you accept the presence of anxiety that you free yourself up to move forward. Otherwise you may waste energy telling yourself that you're bad or weak, which is really of no help.

In Chapter 1 I talked about the importance of being compassionate towards the person you already are. That, essentially, is an act of acceptance. Note that an act of acceptance isn't an act of defeat. Accepting how you are doesn't mean you'll never change – it means you'll stop tying energy up in self-condemnation which could be better devoted to living your life as best you can. And self-compassion might say, 'Look, this is how you are and most of it doesn't matter, but here are one or two areas it would be good for you to work on changing.'

In her book *Acceptance: Passage into Hope*, Sister Miriam Pollard writes: 'I believe that a poor feeling about oneself, held matter-of-factly in the transforming hands of acceptance, can create a person more real, beautiful, and helpful than the person whose emotional world is more secure and uncomplicated.'

That's good news for those of us who know we are

imperfect. When you can accept yourself instead of rejecting yourself this can make you 'more real, beautiful, and helpful' than if you were one of those very self-confident people who you think never experiences anxiety.

ACCEPTANCE AND POTENTIAL

Abraham Maslow, whose work on human needs has been hugely influential in psychology, believed that acceptance, especially of those areas in which we feel helpless or weak, was a vital step towards becoming emotionally mature and realising our potential.

Suppose you think you are a poor conversationalist. Everybody else seems to come up with wittier remarks than you. If you reject this fact about yourself, then the danger is that you won't say anything because nothing sounds brilliant enough. But if you simply accept that you are not a great raconteur, then you will be free to contribute your opinion (and you will probably find that nobody is measuring your wittiness in the first place).

And self-compassion creates the environment in which self-acceptance can flourish. In the example above, if you reject yourself as a social waste of space because you cannot keep an audience enthralled, how are you ever going to get to a point of self-acceptance? But if you are kind towards yourself, if you are a good friend to yourself as you are, then you are far more likely to encourage yourself to say whatever you need to say and to make your voice heard, and from this will come acceptance. You will know that even if a joke falls flat, you will still be your own best friend.

The great counsellor Carl Rogers advocated that therapists should give unconditional acceptance to their clients so that their clients can learn to give acceptance to themselves. Acceptance was a major aim of his therapy and he saw it as a precondition for growth, just as Maslow did.

If I believe I should be the most entertaining person in the room but I know I am not, then I may feel embarrassed and hide. But if I just simply accept without criticism that I'm not an extrovert, that in fact I'm a little bit shy, then maybe I can find one or two people to talk to just as I am. From this I can grow in confidence: I may never become that highly entertaining person, perhaps, but my feeling about myself and my place in the world will be far more positive.

AN ATTITUDE OF ACCEPTANCE

What are some ways of practising an attitude of self-acceptance? It's a difficult word to define but try these:

- If I was to say something like, 'I detest being shy, I hate it, I wish I was rid of it', that obviously is not acceptance. If I was to say, 'Although I would prefer to be confident and extrovert, I am shy and I am not struggling against the reality of that', that's acceptance.

- If I was to say, 'I am willing to have this feeling of anger that is in me even though I don't intend to act on it', that's acceptance of the feeling.

- If I say, 'I acknowledge that what I did in that situation was wrong. If I can, I will put it right', that's acceptance. Note that this doesn't involve beating yourself up about it, which usually doesn't help much, if at all.

- If you say, 'I acknowledge that many people in my life like me and that they are right to like me', that is acceptance of being liked. You would be surprised at how many people find that hard to accept – perhaps you are, or have been, one of them? I certainly have been.

- If I say, 'My body is in pain right now, I don't deny that but I don't demand that the pain go away more quickly than it is going to go anyway', that is acceptance of pain (this doesn't mean not taking medication or not having physiotherapy, but sometimes pain is present even though these measures are taken).

- If I say, 'I acknowledge that this person has been unpleasant to me but I am not going to hurt myself further by recycling the unpleasantness again and again in my mind', that is acceptance of the pain you feel at being treated badly by someone else.

MAKING THE NECESSARY CHANGES

Acceptance doesn't mean taking an unhelpfully passive approach to what you need to change. Instead, acceptance is the indispensable step towards changing what it is possible to change. If I accept that I have a drink problem, then the next question is: what am I going to do about it? If I refuse to accept that I have a problem, then the question becomes: why should I do anything about it? That's one fairly common example of the power of acceptance to set people on the road to change.

Sometimes, though, acceptance needs to be combined with self-compassion to help us do what is good for ourselves. Sometimes a person will accept that they have, for instance, an abusive partner and will then go on to say that, having accepted this, they realise they can do nothing about it. However, if they are self-compassionate, they will not be willing to give up on themselves so easily and they will explore what they need to do to take the first steps on the road to a better life. I should explain that in this example what the person is accepting is the reality of the fact that they have an abusive partner – sometimes people put off this acceptance for years by making excuses for their partner's behaviour and as a result they may endure mistreatment for a long time.

Acceptance should be cultivated always within the atmosphere of self-compassion. Acceptance and self-compassion feed and gain strength from each other.

So think of acceptance, not as something that just 'happens' in your life now and then, but as something you will actively seek to cultivate. Both the practice of self-compassion and the practice of mindfulness – kindfulness – will help you to do this.

Self-compassion and Mindfulness Practices

ONE DAY OF ACCEPTANCE

For a day, experiment with accepting whatever comes your way and with accepting your own self. Remember that this doesn't mean rolling over and letting people walk on you. Nor does it mean running riot!

Bring a quiet mind to events instead of losing yourself in critical self-talk about them. If you find yourself ranting away at yourself in your mind, return your attention to your breath.

Notice that many of the happenings and faults you complain about don't really matter and are not worth getting upset over. Notice also how staying out of that condemning mind makes you far more effective in dealing with the issues that really matter.

One fascinating acceptance trick is to pretend to yourself, no matter what happens, that you chose it. This may seem daft but you will be surprised at how much of your experience you do actually choose.

Who was it who put off driving to the shops until

the evening rush hour? Why, it was you! Try it with your characteristics as well. For instance, if you are a shy person, pretend you chose to be shy and see how that feels.

Remember this is a trick – I don't really want you going around thinking you've made it rain, but it's a very illuminating trick which can deepen your capacity for acceptance.

SPOT IMPERFECTIONS WITHOUT CRITICISM

The old Chinese Taoist philosophers valued imperfection. Take a leaf out of their book. To do this, look out for imperfections – in objects, for instance: the chip on a vase, a scratch on the furniture, a picture that is very slightly askew. Look at them mindfully, perhaps with an awareness of your breath in the background, without criticising them in your head.

Similarly, think of an imperfection, physical or otherwise, that you have and that you can accept and maybe even value for now. See what that feels like.

AFFIRMATION

'I accept this reality.'

When you accept reality, you decide not to struggle against what you cannot change. This can bring about an immediate sense of relief. More importantly, perhaps, it allows you to devote your energies to what you can change and to what is important in your life. Sometimes the reality you're accepting is a feeling, and sometimes it's an event or a person. Experiment with this and see the difference it makes.

REMEMBER THIS . . .

Self-acceptance is the sister of self-compassion. If you are more compassionate towards yourself, you will be more accepting of yourself. If you are more accepting of yourself, you will be more compassionate to yourself. Use the ideas and practices in this chapter to cultivate the powerful attitude of acceptance and see your self-compassion grow.

NOTES

- **Sister Miriam Pollard** is a Cistercian nun and former Prioress of Santa Rita Abbey in Arizona. Her many

books include *Acceptance: Passage into Hope*. More:
www.santaritaabbey.org

- **Abraham Maslow** was an American Jewish psychologist
  who experienced anti-Semitism as a child and who, as a
  response to the horrors of World War Two, focused on
  people's positive qualities and on the drive to realise one's
  potential. His books include *Toward a Psychology of
  Being*. More: Wikipedia has a good outline of his life,
  career and work.

'Compassion first.'

4

THE BENEFITS OF
SELF-COMPASSION

Annalisa's friend Marie is a perfectionist. She puts in long hours to make things come out the way she wants them to and when she fails she becomes restless and snappy. She makes big demands on her team at work and has no time for emotions (though Annalisa says Marie is a bundle of emotions). So when Annalisa told Marie she was doing a course in self-compassion, Marie scoffed. Wishy-washy, marshmallowy, New Agey rubbish, she called it. Not only did Annalisa go ahead with the course, she was delighted to learn that the scientific research about self-compassion was accumulating. She even forwarded the notes on the research into self-compassion to Marie who grudgingly admitted that there might be 'something in this stuff' after all, before changing the subject.

Research matters because it confirms the value of self-compassion and helps to answer some of the questions that trouble people about it. For instance, people sometimes wonder if self-compassion might make them lazy because they know they will still like themselves whether or not they are high achievers (it won't). However, if you are happy to learn about self-compassion from experience and aren't keen on reading about research, by all means skip this chapter. But if you read it, I think you'll find it worthwhile.

The benefits of self-compassion, as confirmed in research over the past 10 years, include:

- reductions in depression and anxiety;

- better relationships; and

- feeling freer to pursue one's goals.

These are benefits that can enhance the life experience of anybody, including Marie, and it's wonderful that we can gain them without doing anything terribly demanding, but by learning to give ourselves self-compassion.

Self-compassion Research

ANXIETY AND DEPRESSION

Anxiety and depression are common symptoms in an age in which we expect more and more of ourselves. Instead, we can give ourselves self-compassion as an antidote to expectations that may not serve us well:

- In general, self-compassion reduces anxiety and depression. In one study, levels of anxiety and depression fell in people who took part in a workshop which featured self-compassion and mindfulness. The more self-compassion practice they did, the greater the effects.

- When asked to think about negative events and difficulties in the previous three weeks, self-compassionate people were less anxious and self-conscious. They were also less likely to feel isolated by their problems, acknowledging the principle of common humanity: many other people have had similar problems so I don't have to feel I am alone in the world in having that problem.

- Self-compassionate people ruminate (brood on negative issues) less. When we ruminate we become preoccupied with negative aspects of ourselves and of the world, and this can then affect our behaviour. For instance, if we brood on some forthcoming event (a fancy-dress party, for example) that makes us nervous, we may become too caught up in our fear to give attention to what we need to do (find a costume we can live with).

- People asked to recall painful past events found the recollection less painful if they had learned to be self-compassionate. This didn't mean they were learning to minimise their part in these events. On the contrary, they were more likely to take personal responsibility than a comparison group (who had high levels of self-esteem).

RELATIONSHIPS

Any fear that self-compassion might lead to selfishness in relationships is laid to rest by research suggesting that the opposite is the case:

- Self-compassionate people have been found to be more connected to their partners but less controlling. They feel more secure in their attachment to their partner. They are less physically or verbally aggressive. They are more likely to compromise when in conflict with parents or partners. In other words, self-compassion doesn't need to be overly defensive and this is a terrific benefit in relationships.

- Self-compassion increases empathy for others and this is evidenced by greater activation in the insula, a structure in the brain that is involved in awareness of the body and in empathy. Empathy means being more 'in tune' with how other people are feeling. It isn't mind reading – there's no magic here! It's about having a greater ability to put yourself in another person's shoes. For us, as social animals, it's a truly valuable skill.

- Self-compassion is associated with social connectedness, support for one's partner's autonomy and a lower level of aggression. Being able to participate in social relationships while respecting the other person's autonomy is psycho-logically and emotionally healthy, because you don't need your partner to go on proving endlessly that they love you, you don't have to cling and you don't have to be continually reassured. This truly underlines the value of self-compassion in relationships.

- People who are self-compassionate and mindful report more happiness, good feelings and curiosity than those who are not. All these make self-compassionate people much easier to live with.

- A Dutch study found that self-compassionate people spent less time comparing themselves to others than those characterised by self-esteem. (As I've explained in Chapter 1, self-esteem can depend on other people's approval and on events that make you feel like a winner, whereas self-compassion does not require that you win or that others approve of you.) Their sense of self-worth was also more stable. And while self-esteem was associated with narcissism (boosting your own importance, discounting the importance of others, believing the world revolves, or should revolve, around you), self-compassion was not – so you can be self-compassionate without needing to be top dog!

MOTIVATION

That self-compassion improves our motivation might not seem obvious at first glance. But by removing the fear of self-criticism if we fail, self-compassion can actually help our motivation:

43

- Self-compassionate people set their standards as high as perfectionists but, unlike perfectionists, they accept that they cannot always succeed.

- They experience less anxiety than others in relation to trying to act on their goals and are less likely to put things off pointlessly (i.e. procrastinate).

- While acting on their motivations and goals they are less concerned than others about boosting their self-image and they fear failure less.

One of my favourite images is of identical twins in a ballroom. One is success and the other is failure. You may want to dance with the twin who represents success but you won't know which one you're with when you start the dance. A complication is that each of the twins can become the other without warning – success can become failure and failure success in the blink of an eye.

If you insist that you must succeed in order to be a good person, if you are going to give yourself a terribly hard time if you fail, then you can't take the risk of dancing at all, especially since you don't know which twin you're dancing with. But, if you're going to be a friend to yourself no matter what happens, then you can make the long walk across the floor and ask one of the twins to dance! That's how self-compassion frees us to be motivated without a guarantee of success.

HEALTHY BEHAVIOURS

By taking a kind approach to the difficulties of changing harmful behaviours, self-compassion helps us in this challenging task:

- Self-compassion makes it easier to behave in healthy ways. For instance, people who break a planned diet often overeat to deal with their feelings of guilt. Self-compassionate people are less likely to respond in this way.

- Self-compassionate people in one study found it easier to give up smoking, especially if they had previously been very critical of themselves. Self-compassionate women who exercised were less concerned about how they looked to others.

When we use overeating, or some similar behaviour, to comfort ourselves if we have negative feelings, then negative feelings, which we all have, trigger that behaviour. Self-compassion gives us an alternative way to deal with our negative feelings. There's more to overcoming unhealthy behaviours than this alone, but self-compassion can help hugely in our efforts to lead healthier lives.

MINDFULNESS

The practice of mindfulness in itself will help you to be more compassionate towards yourself:

- A number of studies show that people who practise mindfulness become more self-compassionate. I suspect this is linked to the increased levels of empathy, which I mentioned above and which are a feature both of mindfulness and of self-compassion, and together become kindfulness.

Self-compassion and Mindfulness Practices

FILLED WITH SELF-COMPASSION

Imagine self-compassion as a light radiating from your heart. Now imagine the light gradually filling your body from the inside. Imagine the light is bringing a sensation of warmth. Just notice that light and that warmth settling throughout your body.

If there are places in your body where you hold negativity towards yourself, imagine the light illuminating those places and filling them with warmth.

Imagine your head, chest, tummy, legs and arms filled with the light of self-compassion. Notice what that feels like.

Allow yourself to rest in it for a few minutes.

MINDFULNESS OF THE MOMENT

Notice aspects of the moment that you are in now. What does it sound like: music, talk, cars, birds, for instance? What is the light of this moment like, wherever you are? Is it a brightly lit moment or a dark one? Perhaps it's dull? Perhaps it's soft? How does the moment smell: pleasant, unpleasant, neutral? What is your breath doing in this moment? Is your body resting in this moment or is it moving along? What kind of emotion belongs to this moment right now?

Try this practice every now and then, to help yourself to get involved in moments. You don't have to be in an interesting place to do it; just any place, any moment.

AFFIRMATION

'Compassion first.'

Compassion here means compassion towards yourself. Try to remind yourself to put compassion first when you are looking at a mistake you've made, judging yourself or, indeed, making plans. Making 'compassion first' part of your thinking can change your entire approach to your day and to your life.

REMEMBER THIS . . .

Self-compassion is good for you. That's a fact. Across a whole range of areas including anxiety, depression, relationships, motivation and making healthy choices, self-compassion has been found to have positive and really helpful effects.

NOTES

- For this chapter I am indebted to **Dr Kristin Neff** for her chapter, 'The science of self-compassion', in *Compassion and Wisdom in Psychotherapy*, edited by Christopher Germer and Ronald Siegel (Guilford Press, 2014).

'I am willing to bring compassion to our common humanity.'

5

THE COMFORT OF OUR COMMON HUMANITY

Many of Christine's most often-used phrases used to begin with the words 'everybody else': 'Everybody else has better luck than I have'; 'Everybody else has more fun than I have'; 'Everybody else has a better career'; 'Everybody else has a house of their own.'

But when Christine became depressed she would switch from 'everybody else' to 'nobody else': 'Nobody else is as big a failure as I am'; 'Nobody else has ever been stuck in a dead-end job for so long'; 'Nobody else lives in a dump like this.' She felt very alone in the world.

This is hardly to be wondered at. If she believed she was different to everybody else, and if everybody else had a far better life than she had, then she was in a very bleak place indeed. Even when she had a success, she discounted it by saying, 'Anyone could have done that'. Not only could everyone else have done it, but, because she was able to do it, well, it counted for nothing.

During a course she attended with a friend, Christine

told me she had always believed herself to be unique. In many respects that was a belief that she had picked up from the culture she grew up in. The idea that you are unique in every possible way is pretty normal in Western culture. The trouble is, of course, that if you fail – as we all do – and if you think you are unique, then you are in danger of thinking that you are a unique failure. That was the sort of thinking that dogged Christine.

With her colleagues at work, with a friend from her schooldays, with the people who shared the block of apartments in which she lived, she had a sense of them being separate from her in her uniqueness. Moreover, Christine felt that they seemed to have a better grasp on their social life, on work and on everything else that mattered. She felt angry about all this and she feared that if everybody else knew how angry she was, they probably wouldn't want to talk to her. The same applied to her feelings about her bouts of depression and her anxiety – she considered these flaws unique to her in her social circle.

One of Christine's big tasks in learning to be self-compassionate is to drop the concept that she is different from everybody else and to begin to see how very much she has in common with the rest of humanity. She can even come to enjoy the sense of being 'just like anyone else', with similar feelings, emotions and problems. In this way, her sense of isolation will begin to fade.

COMMON HUMANITY – A KEY TO SELF-COMPASSION

As I mentioned in Chapter 1, according to Dr Kristin Neff – recognised as one of the world's leading academics on the topic – common humanity is one of the keys to self-compassion.

Dr Neff describes self-compassion as having three components: kindness towards the self; an awareness of our common humanity; and mindfulness.

These three themes are interwoven throughout this book – as 'kindfulness' – and in this chapter I want to take a closer look at the very helpful concept of common humanity.

IT'S NOT ONLY YOU

When you have an issue with self-compassion, it's very easy, like Christine, to carry the burden of imagining that you alone are unworthy or that you are unworthy in your own special way. You can feel isolated in your unworthiness and this isolation increases the pain.

What we need to do here is to understand that the behaviours or characteristics we regard as making us unworthy are shared by huge numbers of people around the world – it's not just you on the whole planet that has this characteristic.

Knowing, and accepting, this can help to break down the seriousness with which we view sometimes minor behaviours or 'unworthy' aspects of ourselves, and it helps to reduce our isolation.

- Do you always leave things to the last minute? So do millions of other people.

- Did you miss out on that career you really wanted to have? So did millions of other people.

- Do some other people in your life find you disappointing? Millions of others also have those in their lives who find them disappointing.

COMMON HUMANITY NOURISHES SELF-COMPASSION

Dr Kristin Neff believes that an empathic appreciation of our common humanity can greatly help us to develop self-compassion.

Perhaps you have, at some time or other, said to somebody when trying to console them, 'You're not the only person who feels this way.' We say this because it comforts us to know that other people feel as we do. What you're being asked to do here is to talk to yourself in the same way that you would when consoling or comforting another person.

The appreciation of common humanity breaks us out of the prison that I call the 'unicorn complex'. We are continually told that we are unique, but that belief creates isolation. Suppose one, and only one, unicorn exists in the world. Suppose you are that unicorn. If that unicorn has faults, that means all the unicorns in the world have faults because there's only one unicorn in the world, who happens to be you.

The good news is that you are not a unicorn. You don't have to imprison yourself in the belief that you are so unique your faults are unique as well. Have you ever done a personality test? I mean a proper, scientifically validated test, not something in the back of a magazine at the dentist? If so, you might have been rather surprised at how well the test was able to describe you. How could a mere test possibly reveal all this deep information about you? Because we are not as unique as we like to think. In my opinion, that's good news.

Sometimes if I'm in a low mood, in which I feel bleak and out of sorts with the world, I find it comforting to remind myself that lots of other people in the world right now – in their homes, at work, in their cars, on the train, at play – are feeling the same way and that all of our moods will gradually change. The same principle of common humanity applies to my faults and to many of my beliefs. Even my belief that I'm special is shared by billions of people. I don't mean that billions of people believe I'm special, I mean that each of them believes he or she is special! One of the practices in this chapter, called 'tonglen', builds on this idea (see page 56).

Try to remind yourself frequently how much we all

share in our common humanity with billions of human beings, all of whom are here, real and on the planet right now.

Even a lack of self-compassion is something we share with millions, maybe billions, of people, many of whom, probably including yourself, are quite compassionate towards others. But each of us can begin to change that so that we become one of those millions who are also compassionate towards ourselves.

Self-compassion and Mindfulness Practices

TONGLEN: BREATHE IN THE NEGATIVE; BREATHE OUT THE POSITIVE

In this old Buddhist practice, called tonglen, which is recommended by Pema Chödrön in her books, we imagine we are breathing in the negative emotions or thoughts of other people in the world and that we are breathing out positivity towards them. This is also sometimes called a 'giving and taking' practice: we take in other people's emotions and we breathe out compassion.

Breathing in rather than breathing out the negative feeling may seem odd, but it's a recognition that so many others feel just as you do right now and so you offer self-compassion (or another positive feeling) to them just as you do to yourself. However, if you find this practice difficult to do, because of the concept of breathing in the negative, it's okay to skip it.

To do it, notice a negative feeling you may be having. Let's take self-criticism as an example, shortening that to criticism. Now, as you breathe in awareness, and recognise that millions of people are criticising themselves at the moment, say to yourself as many times as you would like: 'Breathing in criticism; breathing out self-compassion.'

Another example might be: 'Breathing in shyness; breathing out self-compassion.' Or: 'Breathing in anger; breathing out self-compassion.'

In this practice, then, we recognise that we share our negative feelings with many people in the world and we then offer them the gift of self-compassion, as well as offering it to ourselves.

SOFTENING THE INTERNAL TONE OF VOICE

Many of us, when engaging in self-criticism, speak to ourselves in a very harsh way. In fact, we would be highly embarrassed if we were to speak to anybody else in the same way because our inhibitions were temporarily lowered, by anger or alcohol for instance. And if somebody else spoke to us like that we wouldn't really want to talk to them again.

Dr Kristin Neff has suggested that perhaps we are

so harsh, sometimes even cruel, in the way we address ourselves because it's all happening inside our heads. In other words, there's nobody external present in front of whom we would be embarrassed to say these things, or indeed who might ask us to stop saying them.

One way to begin to work with this is to soften the tone of voice with which you speak to yourself. If you criticise yourself with an internal tone of voice that is hard and harsh – and it can sound surprisingly harsh when you start to pay attention to it – try to pause and to restate the point in a softer tone of voice. Taking that pause and softening the tone necessarily changes how you address yourself.

So instead of calling yourself a 'damn fool' and a 'useless human being' (which is the mild version!) because you forgot to buy fresh bread on the way home, you can soften that down into something like, 'I need to find a way to remember to buy these last-minute groceries in the future'.

So pause and soften your tone of voice, and thereby change your experience.

AFFIRMATION

'I am willing to bring compassion to our common humanity.'

With this affirmation, we extend compassion to all those who share our faults and virtues. In doing so, we're extending compassion to ourselves because we ourselves and our characteristics are included in our common humanity. The affirmation begins with the phrase 'I am willing' because it isn't always easy to extend compassion when our common humanity gets in the way of what we want, for example something you've ordered on the Internet arrives late or the person in front of you at the traffic lights daydreams all the way through a green light. But to be 'willing' to extend compassion to humanity in all its irritability is a huge step forward for many of us.

REMEMBER THIS . . .

You are not so unique that you are alone. In certain ways, you are unique – nobody else has your fingerprint and your DNA is quite exclusively yours. But in terms of your emotions, your thinking and your behaviour, you share far more with other people than that which separates you.

'Today I bring,
to the parts of
myself I do not
like, the gift of
friendship.'

6

BUT WHAT ABOUT THE FLAWED PARTS OF ME?

When Margaret looks in the mirror she sees a very flawed person looking back at her. She feels especially flawed in two situations. One is when she has made a promise that she hasn't kept and she knows the other person is, or must be, disappointed. Margaret has a habit of making promises to end stressful conversations. At work, for instance, when a colleague complains about the stress involved in a project, she is quite likely to promise to take on part of that project.

All too often, though, no sooner has she made her promise than she has forgotten about it, until the deadline looms and people are looking for results. Then she gets down to it but very often the project runs over time. She knows that this is sometimes very frustrating for colleagues who have to work harder to make up for her failure to keep promises and she feels bad about it.

The other situation in which Margaret feels bad about herself is when she has snapped at her children unfairly.

Margaret finds much of the business of being a mother rather irritating and sometimes boring. She tries her best to overcome this, spending as much time as she can with her children. She reads them stories and plays games with them but she also snaps at them very easily.

It's as though somewhere inside her she has a resentment of their endless need for attention. She has an unspoken feeling that they really should be grateful for what they have compared with what she had, which was two super-critical parents, when she was growing up. When one of her children goes away disappointed, or even crying, Margaret feels absolutely terrible. She tells herself what a horrible mother she is, what an awful person she is and how it would be better if she had never been born or never had children, and so on. But the next day she gets up and she tries again and, all too often, 'fails' again.

If Margaret can learn, through the practice of kindfulness, to accept herself as a human being who wants to do her best for her children, even though she is imperfect, she can start to enjoy parenthood. And self-acceptance will gradually remove the need to make herself look better with unrealistic promises to colleagues.

Beautiful, Ugly, Nasty, Nice

Many people, especially if they did not see all the pain this brings to Margaret, would criticise her. Others would give her credit for trying again and again. Margaret would be in the first group: the critics.

We are beautiful and ugly; nasty and nice; good and bad.

We can learn to acknowledge the ugly side of our behaviour from the viewpoint of a good friend rather than that of a harsh critic. Does this mean we do nothing about the ugly side? No, it isn't a question of saying, 'Oh well, that's the way it is. Nothing I can do about it.' Psychologists see acceptance, in this case, acceptance of the self, as a key aspect of self-compassion and as a gateway to change.

THE KEY: SELF-COMPASSION AND SELF-ACCEPTANCE

Self-compassion and self-acceptance foster change. For instance, if I am walking in the wrong direction, accepting that this is so allows me to change direction. If I refuse to accept I am walking in the wrong direction, why would I change course?

In Chapter 1, I asked you to practise being a friend to the person you already are. That's all very well in relation to the good parts of ourselves, but what about the ugly parts? I can accept the flowers in my garden, but what about the weeds? First, let's bear in mind the distinction between a true friend and an abusive critic. How might an abusive critic address those ugly parts of your behaviour? Probably by telling you that you are useless, a failure, a complete waste of space, perhaps a human being who should have never been born. The critic would seek to make you feel ashamed and devastated. That's so emotionally painful that you could be forgiven for not wanting to look at the issue at all.

Notice that point: the critic often seems to be more interested in shaming you than in bringing about a change in your behaviour. It can feel more like a gloating bully than a friend.

How would a true friend address those ugly parts of your behaviour? Perhaps by pointing out that some of the ugliness exists only in your own mind. So if you have that irrational belief that you need to impress everybody around you all the time, the true friend will set you right. Everybody, your friend will insist, is not, in fact, standing in a queue waiting to be impressed by you. Most would much rather connect with the real you. And what of those parts of your behaviour that really aren't good? Suppose you are irritated by your child's need for attention and you deny her your presence most of the time. The true friend might say, 'Look, you are depriving your child of what she needs. It hurts her and you will regret it in future if you continue this way.' But the true friend is talking to you from the basic attitude of friendship and of genuinely wanting what's right for you and for those you love. The abusive critic, on the other hand, wants to attack you, to knock you down, to devastate you.

So the healthy and self-compassionate approach is to

accept yourself as a true friend would – one who sits down with you, if necessary, to have a firm but friendly chat – and to move forward from there. You may feel that this is letting yourself off the hook in an indulgent way. It's not at all. Psychologist and self-compassion teacher Christopher Germer has pointed out that acceptance comes before change. Carl Rogers, the father of modern counselling, was deeply convinced that accepting the other person completely was the forerunner to those changes that needed to happen. In self-compassion, we extend that acceptance to ourselves.

IT'S SAFE TO TAKE AN HONEST LOOK

When you know that you have your own friendship no matter what, then you are free to look at yourself honestly. It's the same as finding it easier to open up to a friendly, open person than to one who is waiting to pounce. Here's a very simple little story that illustrates this:

One day when I had been thinking about and prac- tising self-compassion, I was driving along a busy road in Dublin when a car cut in in front of me. The driver blared their horn and sped on. In the past, I would have cursed the other driver, not once but many times. But this time? To my surprise, because I was in a self-compassionate mood, I didn't feel the need to condemn the other driver to eternal torment. I was able to accept that, yes, actually I probably should have given way earlier and he or she was quite justified in expressing anger.

In other words, I was able to look at my own behaviour on that road and acknowledge it because I knew that doing so would not cost me my own friendship.

SOMETIMES THIS, SOMETIMES THAT

One way to increase your self-compassion in relation to your faults, real and imagined, is to accept that you cannot be all-good and you cannot be all-bad. Indeed, you would be a unique, and therefore lonely, person in this world if you were all-good or all-bad. Professor David Reynolds whose 'Constructive Living' is based on the Japanese Zen approach, suggests we can take a 'sometimes this, sometimes that' attitude to how we are. What does that mean? Sometimes you're ugly and sometimes you're beautiful. Sometimes you're nasty and sometimes you're nice. Sometimes you're generous and sometimes you're mean. Sometimes you succeed and sometimes you fail. But all of the time you are a friend to yourself. You may feel that's difficult if you're 'sometimes this, sometimes that'? Oh yes, sometimes you will be a puzzled friend, even sometimes an irritated friend, but a friend nonetheless and that's what matters.

WHO'S TALKING?

When you find that you are judging yourself, I think the first step is to ask yourself: 'Who is talking?' Is it the abusive critic or is it the true friend? Are you seeing that gloating, sneering face in the mirror or the face of friendship? Listen to the true friend and let the critic pass by without getting caught up in their toxic attacks. Practising mindfulness approaches, such as returning from the harsh, critical thoughts into awareness of your breathing, will enable you to let the critic pass. When the internal critic starts up, come back gently to your breath, your posture or to an awareness of your surroundings. But most of all, make it a principle that, whatever happens, you're not going to lose your own friendship.

The Deeper Problem of Shame

In the remainder of this chapter I want to look at the deeper problem of shame and self-compassion. To begin, let's look at Regina's story:

Regina has carried a sense of shame around with her since childhood. Her parents had been brought up in families where shame was used to control the children and they used the same method on her – it was all they knew. So instead of telling her that something that she had done was wrong, they told her how bad *she* was. To add to her bad luck, the first teacher she had in school also had a habit of shaming children. She would do this by telling her pupils that they were lazy, stupid and would never get anywhere in life. Some of the more resilient kids shrugged off her poisonous talk. Others, like Regina, who were susceptible to being convinced that they were shameful, let her words get inside them like an infection.

Because of what she had been told both in school and at home, Regina made the assumption that she was a poor learner. As a result, she did less well at school than she could have done. In her early teens she met a boy who admired her and the experience was exhilarating. Nobody had ever found her admirable before.

Within a few months, Regina was pregnant. Her parents arranged for her to go to a home for pregnant girls and from there her baby was adopted. After that, her parents had very little to say to Regina. In their eyes, she had proven she was shameful. Regina was now ashamed of her poor school performance, ashamed of having had sex with her first boyfriend, ashamed of having got pregnant and ashamed of having given the baby up for adoption. That all of this happened before Regina was 16 years old made the impact even more powerful. As the years passed, she found that drinking a lot with her colleagues at the weekends helped to cheer her up by lifting that burden of shame – but then Saturday and Sunday mornings generally brought new reasons to feel ashamed.

Any reasonable person looking at Regina from the outside would say that Regina had no need to feel ashamed. They would see that, had Regina been given a more positive view of herself, the course of her life would have been very different for her.

SHAME: EVERYONE'S EXPERIENCE?

My counselling work, as well as talking to people at my workshops and to those who have read my books, has convinced me that shame is a more common experience than we think it is.

Children can feel shame when severely scolded. A young child might just have been burgling the biscuit tin, but the child who is caught and given a telling off in front of the family doesn't have a yardstick to measure their offence by. She may feel so bad about what she has done that she wants to hide her face from the world, and this wanting to hide is a core aspect of shame.

Probably all of us have done things that led a parent or authority figure to say something along the lines of: 'You ought to be ashamed of yourself.' Perhaps many of us still do things that we would feel embarrassed and ashamed about if everybody knew. So, it's a near-universal experience.

JUSTIFIED AND UNJUSTIFIED SHAME

First of all, I think it is important to say that shame is sometimes justified and sometimes not. If you do something that is very wrong and that contradicts your values, then feeling ashamed of that behaviour can provide a strong motivation to change your ways. In this case, shame may be justified, especially if it prevents you from behaving like this again.

But shame is unjustified when it becomes a long-term companion; when it takes on a life of its own, so to speak. This sort of shame no longer needs to be triggered by your behaviour. Instead it becomes a toxic, permanent presence in your life. In this case, the shame is internal – in other words, you see yourself as essentially shameful. How does this work in ordinary life? At an everyday level, you might compare yourself very unfavourably to, for instance, how other people look and what they achieve – like a child standing at a shop window looking wistfully at what he or she can never have. This is a manifestation of shame that is already within you and, therefore, may bear no relationship to how you actually appear to others or to what you achieve or can hope to have in your life.

This was an element of Regina's sense of shame – she saw her siblings as extremely capable of handling the world in a way that she could not. But on reflection she agreed that this was how she saw everyone; in a way, they belonged in the world and she didn't. As far as she was concerned, she would never have a proper job or a proper relationship because of how she was.

All shame is painful, but this pervasive, internal shame is like a pain that we carry with us every day. It is hardly surprising that people with this shame find it difficult to open themselves up to their emotions. Some shame-filled people hide away, eat too much or too little, drink too much, use drugs or cover the shame with emotions such as anger, which is easier to live with. Indeed, probably any emotion is easier to live with than shame. They may also subject themselves to very harsh self-criticism. (Shame and self-criticism are features of eating disorders and I refer to this again at the end of the chapter.)

SHAME AND SELF-CRITICISM

You'll see that I just made a distinction between shame and self-criticism. I want to tease out a little further what self-criticism involves.

According to those who developed an approach called 'Compassion Focused Therapy', which I will return to later in this chapter, one sort of self-criticism is directed at our mistakes and inadequacies. That's painful enough, but the second form of self-criticism is actually an attack on ourselves, with the purpose of hurting, almost like a form of emotional stabbing. In other words, the aim isn't to help us to do better. This extreme self-criticism aims to hurt.

Does that sound extreme, maybe even far-fetched? Well, think again. Consider some of the statements you make to yourself in the privacy of your own mind ('You fool. Do you have to be so useless?' etc.). Don't some of them fall into that second category – the category of aiming to hurt? I have certainly experienced that and it wouldn't surprise me if you have too. And I think you can see how closely that sort of 'attacking' self-criticism is related to shame.

Do you see what a radical and wonderful thing it is to replace self-criticism with self-compassion?

When Self-compassion is Challenging

If shame and self-criticism are part of your personality, you may find it difficult to accept the whole idea of kindfulness: compassion towards yourself. Indeed, self-compassion runs completely counter to shame and to extreme self-criticism.

How, then, can you practise mindful self-compassion? I would say little by little, taking small steps. If you find that shame and self-criticism block you from experiencing self-compassion, start off with one aspect of yourself you can be compassionate about, rather than your whole self. To put it more clearly, if it's too much to be compassionate towards yourself as a whole, maybe you can be compassionate towards a small part of yourself. Maybe you can feel compassion for yourself as a vulnerable child, for instance. Maybe somebody has said something to you that is unfair and definitely not your fault, and maybe you can feel compassion for yourself in regard to that. Maybe you can feel compassion for yourself as somebody who experiences shame and self-criticism. Gradually, you can expand the circle of self-compassion.

Self-compassion for some people is actually quite a difficult thing to cultivate. If you are such a person, take it slowly. That's the compassionate way to approach this project if you find it scares you – it's rather like coaxing a child to face a fear gradually rather than throwing him into a (to him) frightening situation straight away. Also, think of yourself as part of a community of people who seek to cultivate self-compassion and who have to work at it because they have experienced deep levels of shame and self-criticism in the same way that you have. So you are not alone in this. You're part of a family of people. Take small steps and, bit by bit, you will experience a change for the better.

If you find self-compassion hard to cultivate, here are some other ideas used in Compassion Focused Therapy:

- Be willing to accept compassion from other people. That doesn't mean being willing to be patronised by others, to be looked down on by them or to be put down by them. But when people are genuinely helpful, are offering to be helpful or are showing some compassion for you in a situation you are in, see if you are able to accept at least some of that. It is terribly easy to reject it almost as a reflex, but instead give it a chance and see how that feels.

- Be compassionate and supportive to other people and allow this to awaken your compassion towards yourself. This will also give you a more outward-looking view which is very helpful because looking in on yourself and hating what you see is a very painful experience. But do

remember to try to fan even a weak flame of self-
compassion – in time it will grow stronger.

Regina can begin to dislodge the burden of shame by
practising being self-compassionate to herself as a young
girl. She can help herself to cut down on her drinking by
learning to see this as an act of self-compassion. As she
progresses, she can hope to fully accept herself as the young
teenager who was pushed into having her baby adopted.

EATING DISORDERS

The value of self-compassion in relation to healthy eating
is the subject of Chapter 11 (page 137). However, I want
to briefly talk here about the role of shame and extreme
self-criticism in eating disorders and how self-compassion
can help.

If you have an eating disorder, such as anorexia or
bulimia, you are more likely to experience shame than
other people. Most of us experience at least some degree
of shame, but the levels are higher among people with
eating disorders.

What causes the shame? It may arise from extremely
high levels of self-criticism. Self-criticism seems to be especially high in people with anorexia nervosa. Compassion
for yourself and being able to accept compassion from other
people can be seen as the opposite of those high levels of
self-criticism and shame.

In Compassion Focused Therapy, people with eating disorders are also seen as highly competitive. Obviously, competitiveness involves winning and losing; taken too seriously and personally winning might be seen as a source of pride, which is well and good, and losing as a source of shame, which is harmful.

The desire to compete is present, to a greater or lesser degree, in all of us, but people with eating disorders can bring it to unhelpful levels. From this mindset, even the ability to go without food can be seen as a form of winning. People with anorexia nervosa are very good at self-control and this can be a source of pride for them.

Self-compassion helps in the treatment of eating disorders, probably because it counteracts shame. But from what little I have said here, you will appreciate that this is a complicated and specialised area. So while self-compassion helps people with eating disorders, it should form part of a more complex system of treatment.

Self-compassion and Mindfulness Practices

WHAT WOULD A GOOD FRIEND SAY?

When you find yourself thinking today about your faults, your mistakes and what you should have done differently, pause and ask yourself: 'Who is talking now: good friend or harsh critic?'

If it's the good friend, listen. If it's the harsh critic,

ask what a good friend would say and listen to that instead.

WELL-WISHING

Take a couple of minutes now and then, perhaps with your eyes closed, to do this old Buddhist practice:

- Observe your breathing calmly for a short while.

- Now imagine that somebody has sat down in front of you, facing you. This is someone you like, love or admire.

- Imagining that person sitting in front of you, try to generate a feeling of goodwill and well-wishing towards them. Now say silently, 'Be happy. Be safe. Be well.' Repeat this slowly as many times as you like.

- Now imagine that this person is replaced by a second person. That second person is yourself, with all your faults and virtues.

- Observe yourself sitting there and try to generate the same feeling of goodwill and well-wishing towards yourself that you did towards the person you like, love or admire. And repeat the phrase, 'Be happy. Be safe. Be well.' Again, repeat this as many times as you like.

- Then bring the practice to an end and open your eyes if they're closed.

People sometimes find it difficult to wish themselves well, but I suggest you persist and, if you cannot generate the feeling, form the intention to wish yourself well. This is rather like saying, 'I wish myself well, even though I don't feel it yet'. If you practise this exercise a few times over different days with the intention of directing well-wishing towards yourself, the feeling is likely to follow, eventually.

AFFIRMATION

'Today I bring, to the parts of myself I do not like, the gift of friendship.'

When you bring the gift of friendship to yourself, including those parts of yourself that you do not like, then you can stop hiding from yourself. You can look at yourself honestly knowing that you will never lose your own friendship. This is probably why accepting oneself is often the beginning of profound change: we no longer need to deny the reality of who we are.

Remember that this is not conditional. It is not saying, 'I will be your friend for, say, a month, and then we will see whether you have changed or not.' What you need to know is that you are never going to lose your own friendship. That's what creates a space in which to grow and even flourish.

REMEMBER THIS . . .

When you need to change, the true friend is a better guide than the harsh critic. The harsh critic is more interested in hurting you than in helping you to change. The true friend, on the other hand, has your best interests at heart and acts out of friendship, or even love. The true friend you ask for guidance is the true friend in your heart – it's really worth cultivating this friend as an ever-present guide and help.

NOTES

- **Christopher Germer, PhD,** is a clinical psychologist who specialises in mindfulness and compassion-based psychotherapy. He is a founding member of the Institute for Meditation and Psychotherapy and a clinical instructor in psychology at Harvard Medical School. He was a founder, with Dr Kristin Neff, of the Mindful Self-Compassion training programme. His books include *The Mindful Path to Self-Compassion: Freeing Yourself from Destructive Thoughts and Emotions*. More: https://chrisgermer.com

- **David K. Reynolds** teaches and writes on Japanese therapies, such as Naikan and Morita Therapy. His Constructive Living approach is based on these therapies and makes them accessible in the West. He works in Japan and the US. More (on Constructive Living): www.todoinstitute.org

'This moment,
a moment of
kindfulness.'

7

THE HIDDEN POWER OF YOUR
SACRED COWS

Brian was a man given to judging himself harshly in almost all circumstances. He even found it very difficult to give himself credit when it was due.

When colleagues congratulated him on a successful project and bringing them through a difficult and challenging time, he was quite dismissive about it: 'Don't they get it,' he declared, 'that excellence is what you owe to your employer? You are not being paid to fall short.'

Most people would be delighted to be clapped on the back by colleagues. What was different about Brian? The clues were in his history to date. He had been sent to a school where children were expected to achieve excellence – 'getting by' wasn't good enough. If he got 90 per cent in an essay his teacher's response would be that with harder work he could have got the other 10 per cent. That this was a ridiculous attitude (nobody had ever got 100 per cent in the school) had never occurred to him.

As the youngest in his family Brian had often heard his

parents complaining about his older brother's lackadaisical ways. His older brother certainly had an aversion to knuckling down and doing things he didn't want to do. As a child, Brian, I expect, had quickly realised that the way to be 'well in' with his parents was to pursue the sort of excellence that his other brother was not interested in achieving. This attitude – that you must be excellent to be worthwhile – had followed him into his adult life.

Brian needs to look at how his beliefs deny compassion to himself. For instance, he hasn't taken a holiday for two years, apart from a couple of weekends, because he devoted the time to projects at work. Perhaps he actually needs to take a leaf out of his easy-going brother's book.

But to do that, Brian has to retire his 'sacred cow'. Brian isn't the only one to have a sacred cow – I have them and so do you.

SACRED COWS: WHAT THEY ARE AND WHERE THEY COME FROM

In the 'Person-centred Therapy' of Carl Rogers, the father of modern counselling, 'conditions of worth' – or 'sacred cows', as I call them – can drive our behaviour and our attitudes towards ourselves. 'Sacred cows' are conditions we impose on ourselves – usually without realising we are doing so – and which we believe we must meet before we can consider ourselves worthwhile. It's as though, in the back of our minds, we have one of those targets used for practice by archers, only it's invisible and we often forget it's there, but we continue to aim for it.

Conditions of worth are often based on how we understood the demands and expectations of parents or caregivers and of others who influence our attitudes. This truly underlines the importance of developing healthy, positive attitudes, such as the attitude of kindfulness, for our journey through life.

I want to explain the term 'sacred cows'. If you put together the first letter of each of the words in 'conditions of worth' you get 'cow' and, because we hold some of these conditions in such high regard that we spend our lives trying to achieve them, we could say we treat some of them as 'sacred'. So we can describe these 'conditions of worth' as 'sacred cows'. (By the way, sacred cows are a feature of some religions and in using the phrase I am not disrespecting those practices or beliefs. The sacred cows in this chapter are metaphorical.)

Many of these attitudes, of course, are formed when we are still children. When we grow up, we can look at our 'conditions of worth' and decide which serve us well and which serve us poorly. For this to happen, we need to know that these sacred cows are in our lives in the first place. Because they can operate very much in the background, like a program running silently on your computer, we are often quite unaware of them.

CREATING A SACRED COW

How does this work? Suppose that when you are small your parents insist that you must clear your plate at each meal. When you do it, they praise you. When you don't do it, they scold you. Children draw conclusions from such events.

So, according to Carl Rogers' theory, you might conclude that to be a truly worthwhile person you should clear your plate. You have created a sacred cow.

That doesn't matter very much – it's only about clearing your plate, and your parents are doing their best. But suppose your parents give you extravagant praise when you do well at school but are silent when your performance is average or below average. It would be extremely easy to take from this the idea that your worth depends, at least partly, on the excellence of your performance. And it would be very easy to go on from that to conclude that in order to be worthwhile you must perform at a very high level.

This, in turn, could lead you to live the remainder of your life in a very driven way as a high achiever, and to feel worthless if you don't achieve to that level. To want to be a high achiever is fine in itself, though you're a worthwhile human being whether you are a high achiever or not.

It's when you're driven and when the flip side of achievement is a sense of worthlessness that you need to reflect on whether this need serves you well. For instance, have you ever had that 'Is this all there is?' feeling after scoring a success? That might be a signal that you're being driven by a condition of worth – a sacred cow – and that you need to question whether it's what you really want.

QUESTIONING YOUR SACRED COWS

Children interpret what is going on around them and then use those interpretations as ways to guide their behaviour for the future. But their interpretations are often wrong.

In the example above, it may be that your parents were not, in fact, trying to give you the message that you need to be a high achiever in order to be worthwhile, but instead were trying to encourage you with praise, that's all. Your understandable misinterpretation created a condition of worth for yourself.

Understanding this can help you to become more compassionate towards yourself – and towards your parents who, after all, had or have their own sacred cows to contend with.

To deal with these sacred cows in your life, you need to question their 'sacred' status. For instance, if I believe that everybody in my extended family must approve of me for me to be worthwhile, I need to accept that this is unhelpful and unfair.

Fathers, mothers, brothers, sisters all have different personalities, so, by definition, you cannot get the same level of approval from each of them. Perhaps your sister is terrific at sports and tends to disapprove of people who never kit out. And perhaps your brother is like Brian's and only really admires people who devote themselves to having a good time. How in heaven's name can you get the approval of both of them? Equally, if some people in the family are genuinely nasty to you, attempts to gain their approval are likely to be doomed and painful.

But when you realise that approval-seeking is one of your sacred cows you can take that sacred status away. You can follow the approach of the psychologist Albert Ellis by saying, 'It would be nice to get the approval of everybody in the family. But, hey, it's also impossible and that's okay.' Armed with this attitude you can begin to make new, self-compassionate choices about how to live your life.

REVEALING A SACRED COW

One way to reveal your sacred cows can be to ask what aspects of yourself disappoint you. Suppose you get a promotion but, to your surprise, you feel guilty and disappointed in yourself. You may have a condition of worth – a sacred cow – that says you must not put your head above the parapet, but must stick to your station in life; no promotions, no standing out in the crowd.

When you realise what's going on, you can begin to question it. You can ask, for instance, if the aspect of yourself that disappoints you is linked to a valid personal belief or whether it is based on an impossible condition of worth.

A valid personal belief, for instance, could be that you really want to spend more free time with your children but you have taken a promotion that will shred your free time. Seeing this, you can now make a choice as to whether to take that promotion.

An impossible condition of worth would be the desire, mentioned above, to have the approval of everyone – your boss, your colleagues, your partner, your children, your mother, your father, your in-laws . . . It's ridiculous, isn't it? Seeing this frees you up to make choices that are not dictated by your sacred cows.

The change won't happen in an instant – irrational guilt will still make itself felt for a while – but if you are compassionate towards yourself, you will ride it out.

As I mentioned above, dealing with your sacred cows isn't necessarily an exercise in blaming parents, caregivers or other people in your early life. They had to teach you rules and expectations and were also subject to their own sacred cows. If you know them well, you can probably even figure out their most important ones!

But now you're all grown-up, and you are free to distinguish between those conditions of worth that it makes sense to adopt and adapt as personal values, and those others that you can gradually drop. In other words, you can now begin to make self-compassionate choices in your own life, based on the values that make sense to you.

Self-compassion and Mindfulness Practices

GIVING COMPASSION AS YOU ARE NOW

Think of some of the people from whose judgements you derived your conditions of worth: parents, grand-parents, siblings, teachers, preachers, school friends and so on.

Take a few moments to visualise them. To make the exercise easier, choose one at a time. If you like, you can imagine that you are looking at a photograph of the person, or else just imagine the person sitting in front of you. If visualising is hard for you to do, just call them to mind in whatever way works for you.

Begin to wish them well in a compassionate way, speaking as the person you are now and not as the person you thought you had to be.

Use the phrase, 'Be happy. Be safe. Be well.' Try to feel that sense of compassion, but if you can't feel it, just intend to wish them well. In other words, acknowl-edge that you want to wish them well even if you don't actually feel it. Then, if you persist with the practice, the feeling will eventually follow. It may very well be, of course, that you will feel the sense of compassion from the start, but if not, you don't have to let that fact stop you.

By wishing them well in this way, you act from a position of strength in the sense that you wish them well without right now, in this moment, seeking their approval. Remember, the key is to wish them well as who you are now, not as who they think or thought you ought to be.

NOTICE THOUGHTS, 'ADD NOTHING'

In order to spot conditions of worth and other unhelpful patterns of thinking, it's necessary to be able to see our own thoughts without getting caught up in them. Once we get caught up, we get carried away. It's like the difference between standing on the river-bank and jumping into the water. One way to train yourself to stay on the riverbank is to observe your thoughts while adding nothing to them.

Begin by observing your breathing, right now, for a couple of minutes or, if you prefer, observe the sensations in your feet. Whichever method you choose, thoughts will cross your mind as you observe, even after a few moments.

See if you can be aware of each thought as it crosses your mind and fades away, but without becoming caught up in it.

So there's the thought: 'I wonder what I'll have for lunch.' Just observe the thought and say to yourself silently: 'Add nothing.'

'Add nothing' means don't build another thought on top of the one you've just had. 'I ought to have made lunch before I came to work' is an example of a thought built on top of 'I wonder what I'll have for lunch'. When that happens just say 'Add nothing', and return to your breath or the sensations in your feet.

The next thought arrives: 'I wish this was finished.' Again, simply observe, again saying, 'Add nothing.'

Do this regularly for a few minutes to improve your awareness of your thought patterns.

AFFIRMATION

'This moment, a moment of kindfulness.'

This simple affirmation brings together both mindfulness and self-compassion. Whatever is going on, you can at least allow yourself a moment of kindfulness. Even at a time when you are unhappy with yourself, you can give yourself that one moment.

REMEMBER THIS . . .

Self-compassion: terms and conditions do not apply. If you set out conditions you must meet before you can be compassionate to yourself, you might just deny it to yourself for ever. So drop the terms and conditions and give yourself the gift of self-compassion, starting immediately as who you are right now.

'May you be
happy.'

8

MUDITA: PLEASURE IN THE GOOD FORTUNE OF OTHERS

Jackie is an artist who has always wanted to work in the world of art. She has a good job in graphic design and you might well assume that Jackie would be extremely pleased to be in that world. But instead, she is very unhappy. She sees other people's achievements as far greater than her own, and this attitude is the source of her unhappiness.

When a college friend got a job with a top agency with prestigious clients, Jackie sent her a note of congratulations. But she also began to see herself, working for a middle-level company, as a failure by comparison.

When other people within her workplace have a success, Jackie often sees this as a judgement on herself. And she had a real crisis when another of her college friends had a show in an art gallery and even got a favourable review from a national newspaper. When that same friend splashed out on her wedding, she couldn't help comparing it with her own, more modest, ceremony.

Jackie faces quite a challenge in dealing with this problem

which is taking a lot of the good out of her quality of life. A starting point could be deliberately intending to take pleasure in other people's accomplishments. Notice I said 'intending'. Jackie can't change overnight. She can't suddenly be happy and singing songs of genuine joy because a friend does well. But just having the intention of wishing the friend well can be the start of a process that will lead to a deeper change of feelings down the road.

THE PAINFUL 'COMPARING PLACE'

It's all too easy to lose self-compassion when we compare ourselves unfavourably to others, and which of us doesn't do this now and then? A Buddhist practice called 'mudita' can help us to drop these comparisons.

The word 'mudita' is often translated as 'sympathetic joy' and it involves taking pleasure in the good fortune of other people.

What does this have to do with self-compassion? It helps us to break out of the prison of comparing ourselves unfavourably with other people and of seeing ourselves in a more negative light as a result. Taking pleasure in other people's good fortune pushes those negative comparisons to one side and treats them as irrelevant. Think of those unfavourable comparisons as a cell into which we lock ourselves. Mudita opens the cell doors, perhaps slowly at first, and allows us to step outside into the light of self-acceptance.

Comparing what we have with what we haven't got is one of our most persistent behaviours. The tendency may well be hardwired into our nervous system. Think of a child comparing her toy to another child's and either guarding her own jealously or trying to swap it for what she thinks is better.

William Glasser, who developed 'Choice Theory' and 'Reality Therapy', talked about this tendency as one that puts us into the 'comparing place'. Glasser saw staying out of the comparing place as essential to our happiness.

In the comparing place, we become acutely aware of the difference between what we have and what we want. All too often, the result, as Glasser pointed out, is to make us dissatisfied with what we've got. 'Look at my super new phone with its super new camera . . .' 'Oh no, I've just read about this other super new phone with a super new camera that has more megapixels than mine!' So the 'comparing place' influences our feelings ('I am no longer as happy as I was with my super new phone') and drives our behaviour (I look for unfavourable reviews of that other phone or I pledge to get that phone when my contract runs out) as we try to close the gap.

COMPARING, LIKE CHANGE, IS ENDLESS

But this process can go on endlessly because change never stops – it's like a wheel that keeps on spinning – so what we have keeps changing and what we want keeps changing.

When we compare ourselves to other people we are often asking the question, 'Has this person got a better job, better looks, a better family, an easier life than me?', and so on.

When you come off worst in the comparison the result can be self-criticism and disappointment with the self, rather than self-compassion. Somebody else has just achieved your frustrated ambition to write that novel, run your own company, live in that dream place. Look at you, you've let yourself down: what a disappointment you are! If only you could start all over again!

As Sharon Salzberg puts it in her book, *Loving-Kindness: The Revolutionary Art of Happiness*: 'Comparison or conceit is a gnawing, painful restlessness. It can never bring us peace, because there is no end to the possibilities for comparison.'

'Conceit' is a Buddhist term for comparing ourselves to other people and is viewed as a 'mental affliction'. The practice of taking pleasure in the good fortune of others cuts through all that. It takes us out of the comparing place and makes room for compassion and kindfulness in our lives.

THE MISERY OF BEGRUDGERY

On an everyday level, this is something most of us understand already. In Ireland, and in some other Western cultures, people who cannot take any pleasure in the good fortune of others are called 'begrudgers' and are seen as rather tightened up, negative, resentful people.

To them, the good fortune of others is undeserved and the fact that these others are experiencing good fortune means that somehow the world is failing to function properly.

Every time they look around them they find someone else to begrudge – someone who just got a promotion, or new shoes, or anything else positive in their lives. It's as though the happiness of others is stolen from the begrudger.

Deliberately setting out to appreciate the good fortune of others takes us out of begrudgery and opens us up to the positive in our own lives, including self-compassion.

GLADNESS LIBERATES THE MIND

Sharon Salzberg tells us that, according to the Buddha, gladness liberates the mind, and gladness is what the practice of mudita cultivates.

The formal practice of mudita, as you will see in the self-compassion and mindfulness practices on page 99, involves sharing in the good fortune of a series of people whom you call to mind. In fact, you don't have to call people to mind to practise mudita. When you see someone walking along the street obviously glowing with the pleasure of good news, you can silently wish them more of the same. If your partner is humming to herself because she's happy, you can wish her further happiness.

Even if you don't keep up the formal practice, you can make this attitude part of your life by adopting it as an approach to other people's good fortune. In so doing, you free yourself from the trap of comparing yourself unfavourably to others. Don't be like a gardener who stands at the fence staring at his neighbour's 'better' vegetable patch while his own vegetables die of thirst.

None of this means you have to stop functioning in sensible ways. If you grabbed my iPad and ran off with it as I write this in a coffee shop, I wouldn't sit there enjoying your good fortune. I would call the police. Mudita is not the same as foolishness.

Nor am I suggesting that you will never again wish you had done what somebody else has done. Jackie (at the start of this chapter) may always feel that twinge of jealousy every time she reads of another success by her friend who had the art exhibition. But that twinge will pass all the more quickly if she accepts it as it is – a passing sense of loss which, however, doesn't say anything bad about herself or her friend.

If I begrudge the good fortune of other people, then I am backing myself into a corner of resentment and rejection. In that corner, it is difficult to find any sense of lightness and I am probably the one I hurt because the people I resent are, in all likelihood, off living their own lives and entirely unaware of my feelings.

In that sense, the practice of mudita is a true act of self-compassion.

Self-compassion and Mindfulness Practices

MUDITA: SHARING IN THE HAPPINESS OF OTHERS

Call to mind a friend or someone you love. Think of something positive – of some source of happiness in their life or of some good news they've had. Try to feel pleasure at their good fortune. Say silently, as if speaking to them, 'I wish you continued happiness'. Use a phrase of your own if you prefer. Say it a number of times. Really try to feel that sense of pleasure. If it helps, you can pace the phrase with your breathing, saying it on the out-breath for instance, then resting while a gentle in-breath occurs before saying it on the next out-breath.

Now imagine a neutral person, someone you don't know very well. Good fortune enters their life too, even though you may not know what it is. Again, try to feel pleasure at that good fortune. And again say silently, as if speaking to them, 'I wish you continued happiness'. Say this a number of times.

Finally, imagine someone you may find somewhat irritating or perhaps someone you feel a little jealous of. Don't choose someone who arouses very strong feelings, just someone you view with mild negativity. Again, think of something positive, of some source of happiness in their life. If necessary, use your imagination.

Again, try to feel pleasure at their good fortune. Again, say silently, as if speaking to them, 'I wish you continued happiness'. Say this a number of times. Use a phrase of your own if you prefer.

If you find you can't generate the feeling of pleasure at their good fortune, simply form the intention of doing so.

Including that negative person, I should add, doesn't necessarily mean you are wrong to see them negatively. I cannot know whether you are right or wrong. But wishing well to other people helps to create a positive, compassionate space for ourselves also.

Put a few minutes aside on each of the next few days to try out this practice.

SOUNDS FOCUS AND CHOICELESS AWARENESS

To develop mindfulness we often practise with our senses and in this practice we use the sense of hearing. Sound is very evocative – whether birdsong, a car passing by or a voice you know – so it's great for practising mindfulness. Whenever your mind wanders during this practice, label it silently and gently with the word 'thinking' and bring it back to the sound.

- Take a couple of breaths, in awareness. In other words, pay attention to the breath. We take more than 20,000 breaths a day, usually with our minds somewhere else. To breathe mindfully is to pay attention to your breathing.

- Now see if you can notice the sound of your breathing. There is no need to exaggerate it. It's okay if you can't hear it. Just try.

- Pick another sound in your vicinity and move your focus to it for a while.

- Now expand your awareness to any sounds you can hear. Don't choose one over the rest – use a sort of 'choiceless awareness'.

- Now return your attention to the sound of your breathing.

- Now open your eyes if they are closed.

Notice that what you use here are the sounds of everyday life – your breath, maybe a radio, maybe footsteps. If you would rather use music or an audio recording, that's fine, but whatever mundane sounds you can find in the moment are also good for our purpose.

AFFIRMATION

'May you be happy.'

Try the experiment of using this simple affirmation with at least some of the people who come into your mind or whom you encounter in the real world from time to time. In a sense, it involves a laying down of arms; dropping comparisons and battles for now and letting people go their own way, and doing it without harbouring any resentment in yourself.

Of course, you can make this wish to people towards whom you feel no resentment, and who I hope comprise the majority of your acquaintances, after all.

See if you can include yourself when you spot that you are complaining to yourself about one of your 'failings'. If you already know it's a failing you probably don't need to go on complaining to yourself about it. 'May I be happy' can interrupt all that endless self-criticism and might even be a less threatening way to embark on necessary change.

(I am not suggesting you practise this on somebody who has done you a lot of harm. However, if they are no longer in a position to harm you, it might help you to drop some of the preoccupation you may have with how they behaved.)

REMEMBER THIS . . .

Gladness liberates the mind. Resentment and jealousy can weigh you down, especially the simmering kind. They can take up residence in your mind and get between you and the enjoyment of the positive things in your ordinary life as you mull over your resentments. Gladness, on the other hand, is liberating. It is open and welcoming. There's nothing heavy about it. That's why it can be said that gladness liberates the mind.

NOTES

- **William Glasser** developed Reality Therapy and Choice Theory. His approach is based on the view that we are motivated to achieve basic needs, which are Power, Belonging, Freedom, Fun and Survival. He emphasises the importance of choice in our lives. His books include *Choice Theory: A New Psychology of Personal Freedom*. More: www.wglasser.com

- **Sharon Salzberg**'s childhood, she has said, involved 'considerable loss and turmoil'. She discovered Buddhism at university and went on to study further in India. She subsequently became one of the main transmitters of Buddhist teachings to the West, especially regarding compassion. She has spoken throughout the world about compassion and mindfulness. Her books include

Real Happiness: The Power of Meditation and
Loving-Kindness: The Revolutionary Art of Happiness.
More: www.sharonsalzberg.com

'It's only our bombu nature.'

9

OUR BOMBU NATURE: A BUNDLE OF CONTRADICTIONS

Matilda told me that she had always been hard on herself. She was now in her late fifties and this had been going on for many years. Even as a child she compared herself to a neighbour's daughter whom she saw as, essentially, perfect. Elsa's mother, who often visited Matilda's mother, had the same opinion of Elsa and so Matilda's view was reinforced. Matilda invariably saw herself as doing less well than Elsa. The marks she got in school were not as good; she didn't have as many friends; and she certainly didn't have any posh friends like Elsa had. And her family didn't go on the same sort of exciting holidays and they didn't even have a car, whereas Elsa's dad changed his car every year.

Long after Elsa had moved to another country, Matilda continued to be hard on herself for not 'measuring up' as she thought of it. She was critical of her dress sense, of her work, of her social life and even of her choice of partner. Her self-criticism was like an undercurrent that ran through her life. Even her mother had once said that Matilda never had a good word to say about herself.

A CHANGED PERSPECTIVE

All that changed a couple of years before I met Matilda when Elsa came home on a rare visit from New Zealand. Her choice of partner had not been a good one and the marriage had been unhappy. In fact, Elsa envied Matilda who had a stable relationship with a man who loved her. Elsa had also suffered a good deal of emotional upset and had developed a drinking problem which she still struggled with. She was no longer the confident girl who had left and her face and demeanour bore the marks of a life of struggle.

Suddenly Matilda realised, in a way that was undeniable, that she had been comparing herself all this time to a person who was, actually, just another human being. The real Elsa had never measured up to 'Elsa the perfect person'. The effect on Matilda was a deep sense of sadness at how she had treated herself. Looking back on her childhood, she began to see herself almost as a separate person to whom she had given a very hard time. She tried to treat herself with more kindness and she also saw her partner in a new light. But her failure to appreciate herself for all of those years played on her mind and was a source of pain to her.

OUR COMMON BOMBU NATURE

Matilda almost felt as though she didn't deserve self-compassion because she had given herself such a hard time for all those years. What made the difference was hearing about a Buddhist concept called 'bombu' nature. This odd and slightly silly word refers to the fact that we are inherently never really going to get everything right all the time. We're human and we slip and make mistakes – that's our bombu nature.

Matilda realised that her mistake of putting Elsa on a pedestal and her endless scolding of herself were part of her bombu nature. They had nothing to do with any inherent badness in her. And now she was scolding herself for having scolded herself – more bombu nature! Matilda felt like she was running around in circles. It had to stop. She now began to accept that she had been doing what she had always done: seeing herself as 'not good enough'. With this realisation, she began to take a far more tolerant and loving attitude towards herself. Soon, her feelings changed to friendliness towards herself, toleration and understanding.

Compassion includes empathising with other people's suffering and a willingness to help them to suffer less. We see a child crying and we want to comfort her, for instance. When we extend compassion to ourselves we recognise that we, too, suffer and that we want to comfort ourselves to reduce our suffering.

THE PERFECTION TRAP

One of the sources of suffering is the demand that we be perfect or almost-perfect, that we should always do everything really well and that we should only achieve excellence. It's as though we carry a measuring tape around with us, shaking our heads at the distance between how we are and how we think we ought to be.

It's probably easier than ever to fall into the trap of imagining that we must continually achieve excellence: we have fantastic technologies to help us, the world celebrates very smart people who make a lot of money, we have lots of courses and books and therapies easily available and so on. The phones in our pockets even have Artificial Intelligence to help us be ever more productive. So when we fail, yet again, to live up to perfectionistic demands it's very easy to be hard on ourselves and to forget all about self-compassion.

You may question what's wrong with those perfectionistic demands. What's wrong is that they go against our nature as human beings. For instance, we are often driven by contradictory impulses: 'I want to exercise but I also want to sit and watch television', for example.

OUR CONTRADICTORY MOTIVATIONS

Our motivations are contradictory and easily trip each other up. What are these motivations that give us so much trouble?

Many psychologists have made lists of what it is that motivates us. William Glasser, the formulator of Reality Therapy, reduced our psychological needs to four very simple groups: power, belonging, freedom and play or fun.

1. **Power** can include: achievement, dominance, competing or a job well done.

2. **Belonging** can include: being part of a family, a relationship with another person, supporting a particular football team or being part of a national or religious group.

3. **Freedom** can be anything from climbing Mount Everest to taking a leisurely stroll around the block on your own.

4. **Fun** is essentially about play, which is linked to learning (look at children – or puppies – and how they learn through play).

We all have these four psychological needs to a greater or lesser degree – your need for achievement and my need for fun may be stronger than any of our other needs, for instance.

What about survival? Doesn't that come into it? Yes. What I have outlined above are the psychological needs. Behind these psychological needs is the one we share with all other creatures: the need for survival. This includes the need for shelter, for food and for reproduction. If you go every day to a job that you don't really like but that you need in order to keep the roof over your head, you're probably doing it to meet your need for survival.

But take another look at those psychological needs. See how easily they can contradict each other? If you want to be a winner at sports, you will have to sacrifice the freedom to have a long lie-in on Sunday mornings. If you want to care for a family member, you may have to postpone your plans to develop your career. Examples of how our needs can contradict each other probably run into the millions.

Drives and needs contradict each other and trip each other up. And, because we're human, we have these needs whether we like it or not. So that's one important reason why perfection or near-perfection really are unattainable.

I hope this look at motivations underlines why we deserve some empathy and understanding from ourselves when things fall apart. But isn't it sometimes clearly our own fault that things have fallen apart? Yes, and even then compassion might get us further than condemnation: in my view it's easier to learn from experience when you're not shouting at yourself.

ACCEPTING HUMAN WEAKNESSES

The term 'bombu nature' recognises and accepts our weaknesses as human beings. Many systems, including Buddhism, outline what they see as a path to happiness (in Buddhism the path includes mindfulness and compassion). So why not be happy at all times? Because bombu nature means we're probably going to trip ourselves up on the path. I imagine you could sit down right now and write a list of all the behaviours that you have learned will make you happier and healthier: exercise, diet, certain types of work and play, and so on. Then you could mark how many of these you manage to do every day or even regularly. Chances are, some (maybe most) of them don't get done – that's bombu nature.

With that understanding we can approach ourselves with compassion while aspiring to do better. This means hoping to do better and aiming towards it, while recognising that we may never succeed completely. So what's the point in aspiring? Aspirations can take us some way along the path we want to travel. For instance, aspiring to be fit might get you walking more, and maybe eating more healthily, even if you're never going to do that Olympic-level training you fantasise about. In other words, even aspirations we can never fulfil can be really useful in our lives.

To aid self-compassion, recognise that your drives are both inevitable and contradictory. Try to make choices that you know are good for you. But don't beat yourself up when you come a cropper.

And give compassion to your bombu nature.

A MISTAKE? OH, MY!

In the context of our discussion about bombu nature, let's take a look at the irrational fear of mistakes that dogs many of us.

One day, when I had arranged some slightly complicated

changes to an insurance policy, I found myself worrying afterwards about whether I might have made a mistake. You don't want to make mistakes with insurance policies, but in this instance, if there was one, it would have been fairly easy to unravel. It might have meant more time on the phone to the insurance company when I would far rather be doing something else, but it wasn't really all that serious in the grander scheme of things.

Still, I spotted that something more than the practicalities of the policy was driving my worry. What could it be? I realised that it didn't matter whether the mistake was a big one or a small one – somewhere in my personality I had a huge fear of making a mistake at all. It was as though I believed that if I made a mistake I would somehow become an unacceptable person. I would be cut off from the human herd and sent into the wilderness!

But where did my irrational fear come from? My parents certainly never instilled such a fear in me when I was a child. Neither did my teachers at school – they might have punished me if I made a mistake (well, if I got caught!) but I cannot recall them going a step further and condemning me as a person.

I had to accept that the reasons might never be known to me. The psychologist Dr George Kelly of Ohio State University pointed out in the last century that children interpret everything that goes on around them, but that they don't always get it right. These interpretations can then follow them into adulthood. What was my mistaken interpretation?

Who knows? Maybe other kids laughed at me because I couldn't kick a ball straight, but, if they did, the incident is lost to history. And maybe that wasn't it at all.

But somewhere along the line I had grabbed hold of the wrong end of the stick. I had convinced myself that a mistake could see me expelled from whatever group I wanted to be part of.

In keeping with the theme of common humanity (which we explored in Chapter 5), I am quite certain that I am not alone in this. I have often seen other people exhibit a degree of anxiety to get everything right that is over and above the requirements of the task itself. Anyone looking at the sometimes frantic behaviour of someone who has a real fear of getting things wrong can see their anxiety goes way beyond the task in hand. It is as though the thought, 'I mustn't, mustn't get anything wrong. If I do it will be terrible' has taken over both their mind and body.

You can see the difference between that person and the one who wants to get something right just because they want it to work. If it goes wrong, it will not be a judgement on them as a person. It won't be 'terrible'. They want to get it right because they just want it to work and they can more easily devote themselves to the task with calm and concentration.

Such people are, in my view, as effective as or more so than those who make it into a judgement on themselves. Imagine, for instance, that a mother dressing her toddler for a party has the idea somewhere in her mind that she must impress other mothers in the toddler group. Then imagine a mother dressing a toddler solely for the purpose of dressing the toddler. The second mother can afford to take a far calmer approach than the first – she has no judgement to fear.

Well, suppose this mother is a brain surgeon in her day job. Would I still want her to take that attitude? Yes, actually. I would rather be in the hands of a surgeon who is focused on getting the job done because she wants to do a good job, than of one who is using up valuable resources wondering what people will think of her.

Since I realised this myself, I have tried to remind myself that making a mistake is not usually a matter of life or death. Sometimes I say, 'It's not all about me' as a reminder that, while making a mistake might be a nuisance, it is not a judgement on me as a person.

If I fail, I will be just as good a person as if I succeed. And if I succeed I will be no better a person than if I fail. Do I like to succeed? Of course. And I don't like to fail, especially if failing has serious consequences. But the important and comforting point is this: it's not all about me.

Self-compassion and Mindfulness Practices

SPOTTING BOMBU NATURE

Today, spot examples of bombu nature in yourself and in others. Look for small examples, such as being late, being lazy, forgetting something, saying something you wish you hadn't said, and so on. Practise just noticing the examples and letting them go.

Spotting bombu nature in others as well as in yourself can be really helpful. Many psychotherapists believe that the faults that most annoy us in others are actually our own faults that we don't want to acknowledge. So, in a way, if you cultivate compassion for other people's bombu nature you're cultivating compassion for your own.

See if you can spot five examples in other people and five in yourself and then adopt a tolerant, compassionate attitude towards them.

SLOWING DOWN YOUR PHYSICAL ACTIONS

For a couple of minutes today, a couple of times, slow down your physical actions enough to enable you to be aware of them as you do them. We don't have to move slowly to be mindful, but slowness can be a useful mindfulness exercise nonetheless, and many of our rushed, impatient actions are unnecessary and pointless anyway.

Don't slow down to a degree that looks weird to other people. Just drop your speed enough to aid your awareness.

What does this have to do with self-compassion? It

helps to cultivate mindful awareness and this makes you better at spotting instances in which you are being harsh towards yourself. It's so easy to slip into unfair self-criticism, calling yourself names because you walked past a shop you meant to go to, for instance. When you spot yourself doing it you can stop yourself doing it – just spotting it is usually enough.

AFFIRMATION

'It's only our bombu nature.'

Instead of saying, 'You idiot!' or worse, every time you get something wrong, try saying, 'It's only our bombu nature' instead. You've left it too late, again, to check for the cheapest insurance policy, the ice cream has melted because you forgot to take it out of the car, the bus came and went while you were killing time in the shop . . . Really, these are just human glitches, but the critic in your head will want to beat you up for them anyway. Say 'It's only our bombu nature' and tell the critic to hop it. By the way, you say 'our' to emphasise that it's not just you – everybody has bombu nature.

REMEMBER THIS . . .

Nothing's perfect. It rarely matters. I find this to be one of the most liberating thoughts I can have. The people you like most probably have lots of imperfections and you don't really care about that. In fact, you might even find some of them charming. Lots of people have a favourite old coat – well, isn't that imperfect? Does it matter? No. How about you? Don't you have imperfections? Do they matter? In most cases, probably not. So remember: nothing is perfect and, really, it rarely matters.

'Kindfulness is always in my power.'

10

STEP AWAY FROM STRESS AND BURNOUT WITH KINDFULNESS

Andrew has 300 emails in his inbox at work. To most people that's nothing – 3,000 would be more like it, and most of those will never be answered. To Andrew it's a mountain to climb.

Andrew has always set about getting everything done on time and completely. That's an excellent ambition and a wonderful way to be. Unfortunately, Andrew also has more work to do than any one person can take on successfully.

As a result, his aim of getting to an empty inbox has become harder and harder to achieve. What's worse, after many years of battling to do things really well, Andrew fears he can no longer do anything at all. He's tired all the time and he feels irritable. He believes his employers don't especially care about his dilemma. If they did they would stop loading him with more work than he can possibly do without sacrificing quality.

In fact, his employers, he suspects, have a far lower commitment to quality than Andrew himself has. When he looks up the online ratings for his employer he is sometimes appalled by the poor customer service people experience. But Andrew keeps soldiering on and on and on and on . . . It seems fair to say now that Andrew really can go no further and that even he realises this. As the truth that little is likely to change sinks in, he feels a sense of despair settling down on him. He reaches for another document from his in-tray or to do some work on another email in his inbox and pulls back again, unable to go on.

Andrew is now in burnout and burnout takes the good out of work and a lot of the good out of living. Andrew probably needs to get out of where he is working, but first he needs to develop enough self-compassion to help him to see that. Right now, he thinks he would be a failure if he were to leave his job for an employer where he would be treated better. Self-compassion could help him to see that he owes it to himself to do exactly that.

Stress and burnout shrink our ability to see our choices. Sometimes they distort our thinking to the point at which we begin to entertain thoughts of suicide. Mindfulness enables us to step back from the edge and to see what's going on. Self-compassion enables us to make healthy choices from the perspective of a true friend.

THREE SYSTEMS THAT DRIVE US

Before we move more deeply into this topic, I want to look at some of the psychological systems that drive us. We are, in many respects, creatures of motivation. You might not feel that way at 2.30pm, when most people's energy levels slump and they wish they could take a nice, long siesta. But even that wish is a motivation and, even if you don't get the siesta, you might instead watch a video online of a puppy and a kitten racing each other down a slide which is, for your brain, a form of rest. So though you think you are completely drained of energy and with no motivation to do anything whatsoever you have, in fact, been motivated to do something – not a lot, maybe, but something.

Psychological motivation systems, according to research into human motivation, include these three:

1. Fight or Flight

2. Achievement and Goal-seeking

3. Tend and Befriend

That last motivation – 'Tend and Befriend' – is the one we're most interested in focusing on in this book. But it's the other two that we are more likely to be aware of.

'Fight or Flight' is our response to threats. The threat could be physical or social: if you meet a tiger when you walk around the corner, that's a physical threat; if your boss is angry with you and wants to meet you on Monday morning, that's a social threat. When your brain thinks you are under threat it gets you ready to fight it or to flee from it. To get you going, in one direction or another, it sends large amounts of adrenaline through your system.

'Achievement and Goal-seeking' is everywhere in our lives. Everybody in a workplace is seeking to achieve something, whether that's helping to meet the organisation's goals or just earning a living. Even if you're sitting on your sofa unwilling to move to any appreciable degree and you order a pizza for delivery you are engaging in goal-seeking (getting food) and achievement (voila! a pizza arrives at your door). Achievement and Goal-seeking is driven by dopamine, a chemical in your brain – one of its jobs is motivation.

'Tend and Befriend' promotes compassion and taking care of others. It involves the production of the neurotransmitter oxytocin. When a baby is born, for instance, both parents get a rush of oxytocin, which has them tending to their baby's every need – from cuddles and nappy changes to providing food and security. This system is also active when you feel compassion for others or if you feel a rush of friendship or affection towards another. That 'puppy and kitten on a slide' video will get the oxytocin flowing in most viewers. Self-compassion means cultivating that Tend and Befriend system at least partly towards ourselves.

The first two systems can very easily take over from the Tend and Befriend system. That's fine when we need to deal with a threat or when we need to get something done, but we later need to allow space for the Tend and Befriend system. However, as many people will acknowledge, we often fail to do so, especially in relation to ourselves. We need to give attention to that very important system which helps to keep us, and those around us whom we love, in good shape to face the challenges that life presents and to achieve the goals that draw us on. That is why Tend and Befriend is the motivation system that we are focusing on in this book.

Stress and Burnout

Stress is often unpleasant and harmful, though it can also be linked to pleasant experiences. A footballer, for instance, feels stress when trying to score or to prevent the other side from scoring and without the stress might no longer feel an interest in playing. And who would bother getting on a rollercoaster without the burst of stress and fear that make up the thrill of the experience? But stress becomes toxic when it's ever-present and progresses to the level of burnout.

Burnout is usually associated with work. When you arrive at burnout you no longer derive pleasure from your work and you can become rather cynical about its value, and about the workplace and what you see as a lack of support. You also become negative about your own abilities and you can dread going back into the situation each day. Andrew, for instance, no longer gets any pleasure from his work, believes his employer's appalling aftercare service ruins the experience of too many customers and strongly feels his employer couldn't care less. And he can see that he himself no longer performs with anything approaching efficiency.

The effects of burnout are described well by a woman quoted in the Mindful Nation UK report produced by parliamentarians in the House of Commons. She worked in a job she loved but 'there was a culture of overworking, pressure and burnout. I kept going by taking anti-depressants, but I stopped them because of the side effects. I hardly slept and when I closed my front door at night I was swallowed by panic attacks'.

When she began to practise mindfulness, 'a pathway opened up' and, five years later, 'I've taken ownership of my wellbeing and changed how I work'.

Some workplaces are toxic environments which people need to get out of as soon as they find another option. The alternative could be sickness and poor emotional health.

The woman in the example above was in the grip of two out of three motivation systems: Fight or Flight and Achievement and Goal-seeking. The road to health was through her Tend and Befriend system, directed towards herself with the help of mindfulness.

PERSONAL SOURCES OF STRESS AND BURNOUT

In addressing stress and burnout, what we're concerned with is the stress we can significantly reduce ourselves through the practice of mindful self-compassion, or what is known as kindfulness. In this book, we cannot deal with solutions to external sources of stress – if you work for a bully, for instance, you can help yourself by practising kindfulness, but whether you can stop or remove the bully may well depend on factors outside of your control. These include the willingness of the employing organisation to deal with the situation.

What are some personal sources of stress and burnout? Three important sources are: perfectionism; attachments; and running on auto-pilot.

Perfectionism

The perfectionist is driven to get everything right, even in a world in which that is almost impossible to achieve. Do you want to rear the perfect child? Sorry, but your child has his or her own personality, including a tendency to seek autonomy, and numerous other influences, such as the other parent, friends, relatives, teachers and the Internet. Small wonder, then, that, as Dr Kristin Neff has pointed out, research shows that perfectionists are at a higher risk of psychological problems, including depression, anxiety and eating disorders.

An approach based on self-compassion, rather than perfection, would drop the perfectionistic demand instead of striving endlessly to achieve the impossible. To learn more about this, check out or revisit Chapters 6 and 7 (pages 61 and 81).

Unhelpful attachments

Attachments, for the purposes of this book, are ideas you hold onto even if the cost is high, and these can also be a source of stress and burnout. For instance, suppose you are attached to an image of yourself as a person who can endure whatever life throws at them. If you cling tightly to that image, you are likely to remain in situations (unending workplace bullying, unreasonable demands, etc.) that you would be wiser to leave behind – and self-compassion can help you to see that. In other words, you need to be willing to drop an attachment if it's harming you.

But when you are stressed out, that's very hard to see. Stress induces a sort of tunnel vision that narrows your options. Think of a mother in a high state of stress who's looking for her car keys while the children stand at the car door waiting to be taken to school to do a test. As she storms around the house, possibly swearing, sending the cat running in all directions, she may very well pass her keys by. That's because the option of walking slowly and looking around carefully just doesn't occur to any of us when we've been hijacked by our Fight or Flight system. It may take one of the children, who is far less attached than her mother is to getting to the test on time, to stroll in and pick up the keys.

Running on auto-pilot

Mindfulness can help you to see more clearly, not only in specific situations but in general. That can be especially helpful when you're running on auto-pilot.

Let's say you work hard all week and on Saturdays you

stress yourself out still more getting the kids to ballet, drama, swimming, music and football, as well as pushing them to get started on their weekend's homework. If you do all this on auto-pilot, you can run yourself into the ground as one new activity and demand is added to another.

PAUSING TO QUESTION

If you practise mindfulness you will pause – maybe while sitting in the car waiting for the kids to emerge from their music class – for long enough to see what's going on and to ask yourself, calmly, if this level of activity at the end of a stressed-out working week is good for you or your family. If you practise self-compassion, you will allow yourself to cut back on the activities, so that everyone, including your-self, can have a more relaxed weekend. In your desire to do your best for your children (Tend and Befriend) you have adopted a frankly absurd weekend timetable (Achievement and Goal-setting).

Self-compassion allows you to say 'no' to loading more and more onto your shoulders. In a sense, that shouldn't even need saying.

Greg McKeown, in his book *Essentialism: The Disciplined Pursuit of Less*, points out the obvious but often unappre-ciated fact that we don't have to meet every request life throws at us.

He also points out the less obvious fact that creating some space in your life can require turning down good opportunities as well as bad. Sitting on the committee to organise the school tour might get you in with the other parents, but if you're the parent in our example, you don't have the time and you need to say no.

'Only once you give yourself permission to stop trying to do it all, to stop saying yes to everyone, can you make your highest contribution towards the things that really matter,' McKeown writes.

To put that into effect, I believe, takes self-compassion and some courage. I also think it's worth it.

HELP WITH INESCAPABLE STRESSES

Some stress is inevitable. You may face many demands without the option of dropping them. For instance, if you're a nurse in an emergency department, your stress levels will spike many times a day as you respond to the unpredictable needs of distressed patients and their families.

In this situation, self-compassion and mindfulness can be a huge support. Mindfulness can help to calm down your own emotional system as you address your many challenges. And self-compassion can give you that kindness and support that you need and that you may or may not get from others.

Remember the fundamental principle: whatever is going on in your life, offer yourself kindfulness. That is always in your power to do.

Self-compassion and Mindfulness Practices

A PRACTICE IN EQUANIMITY

This practice aims to help you to develop a sense of mindfulness, of perspective, that might be called equanimity. Equanimity means the quality of looking calmly at what's going on without being dragged mindlessly in one direction or another. It's like sitting in a café observing weekend shoppers rushing about before walking out calmly to join them. This practice is longer than the others in the book, so glance over it first to get a sense of its main outlines.

To do the practice:

- Allow yourself to settle down. Notice how you're feeling physically, emotionally and in your state of mind (in other words, is your mind calm or agitated, curious or bored, light or heavy, confident or anxious and so on?). Simply allow this to be, without trying to change it.

- Now call to mind something that is a source of stress to you. It doesn't have to be the most stressful thing in your life, just something that you feel a little bit of stress about. Take a moment to work out what that might be.

- Now become aware of how holding that issue in

your mind affects your breathing; how it affects you physically in terms of tension; how it affects you emotionally; and, finally, how it affects your state of mind. Just allow all of that to be for a little while – no need to try to change anything. After a little while, allow that issue to fade, as best you can.

• Now call to mind something about which you feel positive. Just take a moment to work out what that might be, no matter how small it is.

• Now, again, look at how holding that issue in your mind affects your breathing; how it affects you physically; how it affects you emotionally; and, finally, how it affects your state of mind. And allow all of that to be as it is for a little while.

• Next, recall that stressful issue and bring it back into your mind alongside the positive issue. Hold both in your mind together as best you can. Notice that you are able to be aware of both of them.

• This means that your awareness is greater than either of these issues. It is also greater than both of them together.

• If your awareness was a great circle, then these issues would simply be items within that circle, with quite a lot of space left over. You could say, right now:

- ○ 'There is more to me than this.
- ○ 'This is not all that I am
- ○ 'There is more to me than this.'

- Now, gradually, allow both of these issues to fade as best you can and, once again, check in with how your breathing is; how you are emotionally; how you are physically; and how you are in your state of mind. Then, when you're ready, you can bring this practice to an end.

THREE-MINUTE MINDFULNESS

Among the easiest mindfulness practices of all, is this three-minute mindfulness practice taught by Professor Mark Williams of Oxford University. If you're feeling too stressed or hurried to do longer practices, this one is ideal. Most of us – all of us – can find at least one space during our day in which we can be mindful for three minutes.

You could do this practice sitting in your car before you go into work or before you come home, before you go to bed at night, at lunchtime or even in the shower.

- For the first minute, connect with an awareness of how you are right now. How are you physically? How are you emotionally? Don't analyse. Just ask the question and notice how you are. Without making any attempt to change that, just try resting for about a minute in that awareness. If how you are changes of its own accord, that's fine.

- For the second minute, practise being mindful of your breath at the entrance to your nostrils. Even during a minute, your mind will wander but gently label that with the word 'thinking' and bring your attention back to your breathing. If you dislike mindful breathing, bring your attention instead to the sensation of your feet against the soles of your shoes and, again, whenever your mind wanders gently label that with the word 'thinking' and bring your attention back to your feet.

- Third: bring your attention to the top of your head, then slowly move your awareness down along your body, from head to toe. Take about a minute to do this.

These three minutes, even though it is quite a short time, give your Tend and Befriend system a chance to switch on. If you can do this a few times a day, all the better, but even once a day is better than never.

AFFIRMATION

'Kindfulness is always in my power.'

However stressed you may be, however 'burned out' you may be, kindfulness is in your power. You can always take the time to treat yourself with kindness and this is especially important to do if you are in a state of burnout. When we are under pressure and when we are doing too much, as so many of us are these days, it is very easy to forget that there is such a thing as self-compassion and that we can always give this gift to ourselves.

REMEMBER THIS . . .

Life lived with self-compassion is a powerful antidote to stress and burnout. Even a few minutes of kindfulness can help to remind you of the importance of bringing kindness to yourself and into your own life. And if you think you don't have time for mindfulness or that you don't deserve self-compassion, then you are in urgent need of both.

NOTES

- **Greg McKeown** is a London-born author, speaker and leadership/management consultant whose book, *Essentialism: The Disciplined Pursuit of Less*, has been a deserved hit. More: www.gregmckeown.com

'Today I offer
myself
self-compassion.'

11

COMPASSIONATE EATING

Every weekday morning John hastily ate a bowl of breakfast cereal, swallowed half a mug of coffee and dashed off to work. Often, he ate standing up. At lunchtime he distractedly wolfed down a truly uninspiring sandwich made, in all probability, by a machine in a factory. Dinner was usually a takeaway, which he rotated between Italian, Indian and Chinese.

Food for John was fuel – something to fill him up as quickly as could be; a chore, like putting on shoes or buying a train ticket. Certainly not something to derive pleasure from.

Could this be you? Do you eat without compassion for yourself? Many people do. Eating standing up, distractedly shovelling a bowl of cereal into your face, is the practice of many of us first thing in the morning. Then there's eating a bland sandwich at lunchtime, eyes fixed on a screen. A dismal scenario, especially if dinner is also a rushed affair.

John, as you can see, is among the ranks of the dismal eaters – but it wasn't always like that. When he was married,

John and his wife cooked meals most evenings because spending money on takeaways made no sense when they were saving for a mortgage. In the aftermath of their breakup he began to rely on takeaways, ready meals and snacks because he felt bad and wasn't really up to cooking. What's more, he felt no incentive to get out the pots and pans for himself alone. All of that was all right as a stopgap, but unfortunately it soon became his way of life.

MINDLESS EATING

John had been hearing about mindfulness from a work colleague and he came to one of my mindfulness courses out of curiosity. When we talked about self-compassion he was intrigued by the idea that self-compassion is a practical behaviour, not just a theory that resides in your mind. This resonated with him as he started to realise that how you treat yourself can have a bearing on how you feel about yourself, and how you can find peace within.

John's issue, now that he lived on his own again, wasn't just that he had dropped the habit of cooking, nor that he was extremely busy. A big contributor to his attitude to cooking was his habit of living in his head a lot of the time. John often wasn't 'in touch' with the real world outside his head, including the rest of his body.

This had got worse after his marriage breakup as he ruminated on what had gone wrong and what might have been, if this or that had been different. One of the problems with living in your head like this is that you miss out on many of the details of ordinary life, by which I mean the life you are actually living. These are the details that don't grab you by the collar and demand that you give them your full attention, but that matter because they are part of your life.

Have you ever eaten your way through a meal that could have been a pleasant experience but wasn't because you spent all the time in your head? And what did you gain from that? Probably nothing, except to miss out on the pleasures of your food.

To John, eating had become one of those mundane details of life, to be dealt with when thinking of something more interesting. Breakfast, lunch and dinner belonged to those humdrum aspects of existence to which he attached no importance, and so breakfast cereals and takeaways filled the gap and meals had been reduced to 'time-filling slots'.

SELF-COMPASSION: PRACTICE, NOT THEORY

But John found the concept of self-compassion, which he had read about somewhere, probably while hurriedly eating, appealing and when we got to that section of the course, he perked up. What he found appealing, I deduced, was not so much self-compassion itself as the idea of it – which differs from the real thing in the same way that the idea of going for a run is different to actually going for a run. If self-compassion was nothing more than a theory, nothing would have changed in John's world outside the course.

However, as soon as he took on board the view that self-compassion is expressed in practical ways, and that clicked for him, his eating habits changed. He bought good ingredients on his way home from work and he cooked tasty meals for himself. He found a decent café near his office and he had lunch there a few times a week, sometimes with a colleague. Suddenly food played a much more important role in his life. In fact, you could argue that it was bringing him back to life.

What really intrigued me was that other aspects of his behaviour also changed. John even went out and bought himself some new clothes, to the puzzlement of his ex-wife who wondered if he had found a girlfriend.

But, sadly, John drifted back to his old ways. Once again he was eating cheap sandwiches and rushed breakfast cereals, and fast food or takeaway meals became the norm again.

ARE YOU WORTH COOKING FOR?

What had gone wrong? When we discussed this turn of events, John's basic feeling that, really, he wasn't worth standing over a cooker for, came to the surface. 'Why bother, if it's just for me?' he asked with a shrug.

I caught a glimpse of sadness in John's reply. He seemed to say it as though he didn't care, but he wasn't smiling. The impression I got was that he was sad at having nobody else to eat with at home and that this had taken the fulfil-ment out of cooking.

But was he terribly unusual in his approach? I don't think so. Most of us are used to the idea of the preparation of meals as a form of caring as well as a way to satisfy hunger. Unless we have been unlucky, we got that idea in childhood when somebody who cared about us cooked a meal and put it on the table in front of us. Even if our parents didn't get to cook for us themselves every day, the preparation of meals, when they could manage it, was an act of caring.

What's wrong with seeing cooking as caring? Nothing. Indeed, to me the real magic in the kitchen happens when cooking is combined with caring. The danger, however, lies in seeing cooking as a means of caring for others but not for oneself. At an extreme, a parent may prepare enjoyable meals for the family but eat nothing him- or herself. At far less of an extreme, when a person lives alone, the whole idea of getting involved with pots and bowls and washing up can seem, well, not worth it.

That's okay when you're pressed for time, are so tired you can't face it or you feel like giving yourself a treat – tucking into a takeaway with one eye on the television. But it's not okay when the idea that you're not worth it lies behind your behaviour.

For John, this was an eye-opener. He had not previously been aware of his own lack of self-worth and how that manifested itself in his attitude to food. He also saw how the same attitude coloured his approach to clothes, to spending on things he liked and to seeking or creating better conditions for himself at work. He deprived himself because, somewhere in his heart, he believed he wasn't worth treating well.

GOOD EATING AS AN ACT OF SELF-COMPASSION

John agreed to eat well – not expensively, but well – as a way to assert his self-worth. He began to regain that feeling of self-worth that had been missing since his marriage breakup, to see that it did not depend on being a winner, or on getting everybody's approval as he had previously thought. Instead, he saw self-worth as a feeling he could cultivate through the practice of self-compassion, providing an environment in which his self-worth could flourish.

What about you? Are you worth cooking for when you're on your own? Think about that seriously because it can tell you a lot about your own sense of self-worth.

If most of your meals are takeaways, why is that? Is it because you like the food? Or is it because you feel that to put all that effort into cooking a pleasant meal for yourself isn't worth it? If that's why the takeaway delivery people in your district could find their way to your door with their eyes shut, then perhaps you should think again. In particular, consider what that tells you about your degree of self-compassion, or the lack of it. The self-compassion and mindfulness practices below will help you to explore that issue and perhaps learn some valuable lessons from it.

If you don't already, start the practice of cooking for yourself or of buying nutritious meals in a pleasant setting as an act of kindfulness. Talking of buying, you could also do your food shopping in a self-compassionate way, not just throwing items into your basket because they're quick to prepare, but instead asking if you would serve this up to a welcome guest. Try it and see what your feelings are as you take the trouble to look after yourself as the welcome guest at the table.

You may be surprised when you see how this helps to begin to bring about a change in that all-important relationship – the one you have with yourself. And you will eat more nutritiously and, very possibly, more cheaply.

Self-compassion and Mindfulness Practices

A MEAL WITH SELF-COMPASSION

Take the time to make a healthy meal for yourself with the same care you would devote to preparing food for a guest. Look up a simple, tasty recipe, get the ingredients and, once you have prepared the meal, take your time eating it. Sit down to eat (no wandering around with a fork and a tin of beans). Enjoy each mouthful and think about the good it is doing you – not just in terms of nutrition but in terms of taking time out for yourself.

Your aim is to cook and/or eat as if you are worth cooking for or buying delicious food for. See if this attitude spreads out from your meal to other parts of your day or evening.

Too busy to do this every evening? Choose the evening of a day off to get started. Then add more evenings as you get used to mindful eating.

A MINDFUL EATING PRACTICE

Mindful eating means being aware that you are eating, of the taste of the food and, indeed, of the whole experience. Some people practise eating food mindfully by sniffing it and rolling it around in their fingers. Yuck! Not for me.

To eat mindfully, be aware of the fact that you are eating while you are eating. That's the fundamental instruction. Notice the taste. When your mind wanders, bring it back to your eating. You'll be surprised at how much your mind will want to wander, by the way. You don't have to eat slowly, just at a pace that allows you to be aware of what you are doing. That's it, and it can greatly increase the pleasure you get from your food. This also happens to be a really pleasant way to cultivate mindfulness.

AFFIRMATION

'Today I offer myself self-compassion.'

This is a phrase to use at the very start of your day and you can repeat it later during the day if you find it helpful. Using it at the start of the day sets you up, so to speak, to take a more friendly attitude towards yourself from the time you get up and out of bed. It also helps you to remember that self-compassion is something you deliberately cultivate, in this case by offering it to yourself. Like mindfulness, self-compassion is a skill and, the more you practise it, the better you will get at making it part of your life. Try using the phrase either before you get out of bed in the morning or as soon as your feet touch the floor.

REMEMBER THIS . . .

Self-compassion is a choice you are free to make. It isn't handed down from on high, you don't have to pass a test to be allowed to use it and you don't have to wait for a moment of enlightenment. Eating pleasant meals with awareness and cooking them for yourself is a delightful way to practise self-compassion in your life and a really good way to treat yourself with kindness.

'How does this
help me?'

12

HOW SELF-COMPASSION MAKES
HEALTHY RELATIONSHIPS

Jason had come to a course in one of a large number of last-ditch attempts to save his marriage. According to Jason, his wife continually criticised and attacked him. 'Nothing I do is right,' he complained. This had been going on for years.

Jason often responded by shutting the argument down: when his wife began with the criticisms he would simply walk out of the room. Things had gone from bad to worse with his wife complaining that he never listened to her and did not care. Jason, on the other hand, maintained that he cared desperately. That was what had prompted him to come on the course.

When we looked at self-compassion and relationships Jason said that he had never been very good at relationships in the past. 'I was just never much good at handling them,' he said.

It struck me that Jason suffered from a characteristic of many very self-critical people: they assume that others, especially their romantic partners, are just as critical of them as they are of themselves. Sometimes this assumption can kick in even when all that's happening, from the other person's point of view, is a normal remark about everyday matters.

For instance, Jason normally did the family shopping at the weekend. If his wife said to him during the week, 'Could you get some milk on the way home because you didn't include it in the shop on Saturday?' he saw this as an attack on him rather than just a request for milk.

I had no doubt, from what he told me, that Jason's wife was more critical than the average person, though not in any sort of abusive way. But I also had no doubt that Jason's self-critical nature inflated annoying criticisms into, in his imagination, major attacks.

His most recent reaction to this, as I have mentioned above, was to walk out of the room when his wife, as he put it, 'starts going on at me'. The problem with this approach is that when one partner refuses to listen to the other – stonewalls them, so to speak – the relationship is close to breaking down altogether. This has been established in research that I will explain later (page 151).

When Jason began to practise self-compassion, he found it easier to stay in the room and listen to his wife instead of walking out. When this happened, things began to change for the better. Jason found that his wife needed to be listened to more than she needed to be agreed with, and that was a big revelation to him. Ultimately, he asked his wife to moderate her too-ready criticisms and she agreed to try if he stayed put and listened to her when she had something she wanted to say. As a result, the bad feeling between them after a row faded more quickly than on previous occasions. By the time Jason had finished the course, he was hopeful that his marriage would be saved.

SELF-COMPASSION: MAKING HEALTHY RELATIONSHIPS

Self-compassion makes us better listeners even when we don't like what we are hearing. That's because the more secure we feel in ourselves the less scared we are by our partner's criticisms. And since self-compassionate people are less likely than self-critical people to assume their partner is attacking them, they allow a greater space for the airing of differences. In this way, self-compassion contributes greatly to the resilience of long-term relationships because, in most cases, differences form part of such relationships.

The 'self' in self-compassion might lead some readers to a fear that cultivating this quality could make a person selfish in relationships. They can imagine themselves saying, insufferably, 'I don't care what you think because I'm okay with myself.'

On the contrary, self-compassion has a great deal to offer to creating and maintaining healthy relationships. It makes partners more open to listening to each other's needs and increases satisfaction in relationships. Self-compassion makes it easier to listen and easier to change. When we're self-compassionate we don't have that voice whispering, 'I wouldn't listen to that if I was you. Besides, if you agree, you'll never hear the end of it.' Self-compassion says, 'No, it's okay and I know I will still be a friend to myself at the end of this, even if I hear I'm not perfect, which I knew already.'

Some relationships have little or no conflict, probably because both partners are similar to each other and are not given to conflict in any aspect of their lives. These relationships are in a small minority, however, so I'm afraid yours is probably not one of them.

Disagreement and conflict are inevitable in almost all long-term relationships. For some of us navigating this conflict is not something that we always manage successfully.

When we lack self-compassion, managing conflict gets even more difficult. For instance, self-compassion researcher Dr Kristin Neff points out that people who are very critical of themselves tend to assume that others are just as critical of them.

Why would they make that assumption? In my view, if we are very critical towards ourselves we set ourselves up to believe the worst because we already judge ourselves by a critical standard. Others might be using an entirely different standard because they see the good in us that we find it hard to see in ourselves.

All this – being quick to take offence – makes matters

worse, and can do so very quickly, when the self-critical person is reacting to non-existent hostility on the part of their partner. That reaction in itself can then lead to the partner becoming hostile. And so, matters go from good, to bad, to worse.

For instance, if one partner is annoyed about an incident at work but hasn't said so, the self-critical partner is very likely to think that the partner's obvious annoyance is related to him or her. Instead of asking 'What's up?' the self-critical partner may say something like, 'I'm sick of you coming in here like a bear with a sore head. You're not so perfect yourself, you know.' Next comes a flurry of door-banging and sulking on both sides. Too much of this can gradually sink the relationship, especially if the couple then neglect to have a reasonable discussion about what just happened (which will go better, I should add, if people have the discussion when everybody has calmed down).

LISTENING TO WHAT WE DON'T WANT TO HEAR

Research by John and Julie Gottman, who have studied marriages in the US over many decades, has found that when one partner simply won't listen to another – 'stonewalls' them, in other words – the marriage is in danger.

If you are very self-critical, you may rush to shut out the other person's views because they will cause you too much pain. 'Here she/he goes again' you say to yourself as the other person's frustration escalates due to your lack of response. A self-compassionate person knows that they will at least be receiving compassion from themselves by the end of the exchange so they feel less need to shut off the other person. In this way, self-compassion opens up the conversation. You could think of this as self-compassion 'on the battlefield' where it can de-escalate conflict.

So self-compassion, by making it easier for us to listen to what we do not want to hear, can reduce both the immediate and long-term damage that can be done by how we handle conflict in relationships.

And this matters. The Gottmans' research shows that some of the issues which annoy partners at the start are 'perpetual' so the need for self-compassion never really goes away! In case you're wondering, perpetual problems can range from one partner being tidier than the other to differences over how the children should be raised. Indeed, even if the relationship breaks down, self-compassion can still help to soothe the wounds. After all, some of those perpetual differences, say over the children's education, survive the breakdown of the relationship.

ADDING POSITIVITY AND
SELF-COMPASSION

I realise that in this chapter so far I may have taken a somewhat gloomy view of the relationship landscape – painting it more as a field of battle than a flowery garden.

But of course it's not all about the downside of long-term relationships.

Self-compassion helps make relationships better. In a study of more than 100 couples, Dr Kristin Neff and Tasha Beretvas (a professor in educational psychology) found that self-compassionate people were happier in their relationships and their partners found them to be more affectionate. They were also able to give their partners more freedom in the relationship. So self-compassionate partners don't sit there admiring themselves in the mirror all day long. On the contrary, they are more likely to be involved in a positive way in the give-and-take of relationships.

Those who lacked self-compassion tended to be more inflexible, critical and controlling. Anyone would be forgiven for thinking that these people lack compassion for others but it turns out that they have too little compassion for themselves. Elsewhere I have mentioned that fear I have heard expressed by so many: 'If people knew what I was really like they wouldn't want to have anything to do with me.' That, I think, is one of the dynamics that excessively controlling people bring to relationships. Sometimes the controlling gets so bad that the controlled person needs to develop enough compassion for themselves to leave.

But where both partners have a healthy liking for themselves as well as each other, the picture is completely different. 'Self-compassion fosters feelings of mutuality in relationships so that the needs of self and other are balanced and integrated,' Dr Kristin Neff writes in her book, *Self Compassion: Stop Beating Yourself Up and Leave Insecurity Behind*. She adds later that 'self-compassion embraces imperfection with love, providing the fertile soil needed for romance to truly flourish'.

Of course, our important relationships include people other than a spouse or partner. Many of us have children, many have relatives we care for and sometimes we have both, as in having a child with a serious disability. But what if all your compassion and caring is for somebody who needs it so badly that you feel guilty about giving compassion to yourself – perhaps someone with a chronic illness?

Christopher Germer points out in his book *The Mindful Path to Self-Compassion: Freeing Yourself from Destructive Thoughts and Emotions*, that 'embracing ourselves during hard times protects us from fatigue and resentment and gives us the energy to be present for others'.

Self-compassion has been found to promote better relationships between those in the caring professions and those they care for. A Canadian study, for instance, has found that medical students with higher levels of self-compassion liked 'difficult' patients more than did those students who were less self-compassionate. 'Compassion-fatigue', characterised by a fall in empathy and a feeling of emotional exhaustion due to excessive workloads, is a risk faced by those who work in caring professions. The accumulating evidence that self-compassion can help to combat compassion-fatigue is highly encouraging.

Self-compassion is needed all the more by those who care for a family member and who are 'on duty' 24 hours a day. For them, it can be very difficult to attend a training course, but the practices in this book could make a huge difference to how they feel and in situations where caring comes to an end.

Sometimes, carers find it difficult to direct self-compassion to themselves within a relationship. In such a case, Christopher Germer suggests, they could use an affirmation such as, 'Just as I wish that my daughter be safe and happy, so may I be safe and happy'. Putting someone else first in the affirmation can help them over the psychological barrier that makes it hard for them to wish well to themselves.

Outside the whole area of caring and sickness, many parents run themselves to a frazzle, especially if they are expected to be perfect fathers or mothers and perfect employees all at the same time. It's all too easy to be 'on the go' during every waking minute and to become worn out and irritable. Self-compassion can help parents to take healing moments for themselves now and then. It's also a great example for the children. If you're a frazzled parent be sure to read Chapter 13 (page 161).

So self-compassion, far from encouraging selfishness in relationships, can actually lead to healthy and honest relationships in which everybody's legitimate needs are met.

Self-compassion and Mindfulness Practices

LEAVE THE STRUGGLE SWITCH OFF

Sometimes what's needed to bring a little ease into our relationships is to stop struggling with every single issue that comes up. That's a way to be compassionate to ourselves and to the other person.

The 'struggle switch' is a metaphor from 'Acceptance and Commitment Therapy' (Dr Russ Harris's *The Happiness Trap* is a good and very readable guide to Acceptance and Commitment Therapy). Imagine you have a switch in your brain called a 'struggle switch'. When it's on, you struggle even when it's completely pointless to do so. For instance, you can get into a big argument with another person over something that really doesn't matter in the least, for example who finished the marmalade and didn't buy more? We've all been there.

Deliberately practise leaving the struggle switch off when it comes to differences with other people that don't really matter. Some differences matter and some don't: it's the ones that matter that deserve your attention.

So to be compassionate towards yourself and others – leave the struggle switch off more often than you keep it on.

UNRESOLVED ISSUES

In every long-term relationship, people have unresolved issues – past mistakes, things done or not done – that disturb the emotions. But many of these issues will never be resolved and continuing to go over and over them simply hurts, and perhaps even damages the relationship.

Could you list some issues you could actually let go of, issues that might have been irritating at the time and that can still annoy you when you think about them, but that you don't really need to hold onto? Could you decide no longer to go over and over these issues in your mind, perhaps even saying 'letting go for my sake' every time you think of them?

This is really worth trying – self-compassion can enable you to accept that many of your issues will never be resolved and instead to bring your energy to your life in the present moment.

AFFIRMATION

'How does this help me?'

When we have the habit of talking to ourselves in a very uncompassionate, self-critical way, and when that has become almost a reflex response if things go wrong, it's very easy to get deep into self-attacking behaviour before we realise it. If you can get into the habit of asking quietly, whenever you notice that this is going on, 'How does this help me?' you'll begin to see what's happening and you will learn to interrupt that destructive pattern of thought. Practise that and see the results.

REMEMBER THIS . . .

Self-compassion can make your relationships bloom. Knowing you have your own friendship, no matter what, increases your level of self-compassion. This helps you to be less touchy and reactive and can work wonders by opening up spaces in which it is safe to talk about some differences and to tolerate others. And that's an essential part of the work that must go into long-term relationships.

NOTES

- **John and Julie Gottman** have conducted decades of research with couples in the US. In many cases they have tracked couples from the beginning to the end of their marriages. Their books include *Why Marriages Succeed or Fail: And How to Make Yours Last*.
  More: www.gottman.com

- **Dr Russ Harris** is a medical practitioner who became a psychotherapist and life coach. He has made mindfulness-based Acceptance and Commitment Therapy very accessible, especially through his book *The Happiness Trap*. More: www.actmindfully.com.au

'Today I am a good enough parent.'

13

SELF-COMPASSION AND 'GOOD ENOUGH' PARENTING

People notice that Kevin, who is a single parent, snaps at his children when they seek his attention. He seems short-tempered and preoccupied when they are around. His sister, Janice, wonders if she should say something but she's reluctant to put him under more pressure than he already feels. Finally, Kevin shouts at his six-year-old in the middle of her birthday party. She runs off in tears. Janice comforts the child, gets her laughing again and saves the day. The next morning, she calls round to have the conversation she knows she has to have.

Janice doesn't accuse Kevin of being a bad parent. Putting him on the defensive immediately will get her nowhere, and she knows Kevin would do anything for his children in spite of his harsh words. Instead, she begins by telling him how much she knows he loves his kids. Then she tells him what else she sees: that he looks irritated when he's around them, that he turns away or barks at them when they demand attention. That someone who didn't know him would think he regarded them as a nuisance.

Kevin's tears really surprise her. He says that he wants to do his best by his children but he fears he is not up to the job. When he meets one demand many others come along and he's afraid he just can't keep up with the innumerable requirements of parenting. Whenever they ask for something new he fears that whatever he does will not be 'good enough'. It was all getting too much and he was doubting, more and more, his own ability as a father.

WHY PARENTS NEED SELF-COMPASSION

Many mums and dads find it next to impossible to keep up with the demands that come with being a parent. Lots of parents find it challenging to meet the vast requirements of parenting. It isn't easy to be boss, parent, playmate, teacher and confidante all at once. Parents learn 'on-the-job'. What you've learned today won't necessarily work next year, or maybe even next month, as your child develops. And, if you have another child, he or she may have a personality so different from the first one that you feel you've got to start learning all over again.

The way you were parented as a child will influence your own parenting style, but it's not the same as training to be a parent. Kevin's sister was seven years older than him so it sometimes felt like he had three parents taking care of him. Kevin's children were close in age – he and his wife had planned it that way before she died. But Kevin didn't have lots of knowledge to bring from his childhood into his parenting, after all, which of us, as a child, is taking notes on parenting as we grow up?

Kevin is doing what lots of very stressed parents do – he's setting the bar too high. He's trying to be perfect in the middle of a messy, muddled, ever-changing situation. It's an impossible demand and it can leave parents stressed out, frazzled and snappy.

That's why parents need self-compassion. But 'Why?' you might ask. Isn't it compassion for your children that matters rather than compassion for yourself?

The fact is that the way you express your compassion for your children can be strongly influenced by the compassion you have for yourself or by the lack of it. Looking after yourself, being kind to yourself and practising kindfulness will make you better able to deal with the ups and down of looking after children, big or small.

That's because your lack of confidence makes it more difficult to get in touch with the more soothing side of your emotional system. Why? Because ruminating on your faults and shortcomings, or worrying about what may happen next or about getting other people's approval, can so easily block that soothing side. And self-compassion is closely connected with your ability to soothe yourself, as I explained earlier (Chapter 10, page 121).

A Portuguese study illustrated a fascinating link between

anxiety, parenting and self-compassion. Researchers examined the experiences of 290 mothers of children aged 8–19 years. What they found was that the more anxious mothers had less self-compassion. Also, they were less mindful. In other words, their awareness was less likely to be in the present moment.

Self-compassion and Mindful Parenting

What does being a mindful parent mean?

Let me begin by emphasising that we are not trying to achieve perfection in parenting or, indeed, any other area of our lives. Instead we are exploring how self-compassion can, in itself, contribute to what is called 'good enough parenting'. The phrase was coined by the psychoanalyst and paediatrician Donald Woods Winnicott who believed that a perfect parent could actually leave a child ill-equipped to deal with the real world. He was all in favour of parents meeting their children's needs – it was overdoing it by never allowing the child to feel frustration that he thought was a bad idea.

So with that caveat – that perfection is not desirable even if it was possible – let's go ahead anyway and look at what being a mindful parent means. It has three main components:

1. A good moment-to-moment awareness of yourself and your child.

2. Being 'present' in your interactions with your child. In today's distracted age, this might be the biggest challenge for most of us as we check work emails or news headlines on our smartphones, for instance, while playing with our child.

3. Bringing sensitivity, kindness and compassion to addressing your child's needs.

See what I mean about perfection?

In practice, though, I think it's easier than it sounds. Putting these three components into practice involves:

- giving your full attention to your child when listening to him or her;

- taking an accepting attitude towards your child in these interactions;

- being aware of your child's and of your own feelings;

- being able to contain your own emotions if necessary (for instance, containing your anger within fair limits);

- choosing to be compassionate towards yourself as well as towards your child.

Now, this isn't like a checklist that you have to run through in your head a hundred times a day. Try that and you'll spend your day going through checklists while your child protests. It's more about the quality of your relationship with your child and yourself.

LACK OF CONFIDENCE AND ANXIETY

But doesn't all this come naturally to you? No, it doesn't. Before you have children your only experience of parenting comes through being a child and that's looking through the wrong end of the telescope! Recognising this is the start of self-compassion for yourself as a parent.

But the lack of confidence that can assail parents, especially new parents, isn't just about not knowing what to do with this creature who has just come into the world or, maybe, who has just arrived at adolescence.

For instance, if you lack confidence about your ability to meet other people's needs, then your child can unintentionally trigger anxiety and distress by expressing his or her own needs. This is what was happening with Kevin. When he worked full-time, Kevin felt very confident in what he did. But outside of the world of work he had never really felt all that confident in his relationships with other people. This lack of confidence also applied to his relationship with the demanding little people in his own home.

Ruminating on his fears and lack of confidence made it worse. Preoccupation with anxieties often results in rumination, as I mentioned above, and rumination is a great enemy of mindfulness. When you ruminate, you follow your negative thoughts around and around in circles. This boosts the activity of your Fight or Flight system. That in turn hijacks your attention and stops you from being mindful.

Lost in rumination, you may snap at your child when he or she pulls you out of it with even a simple question or by knocking something over.

But the practice of mindfulness can reduce rumination and can make it much easier for you to step into awareness of the present moment. That's one of the ways in which mindfulness helps us to cultivate self-compassion.

Remember, you need to find ways to make mindfulness a habit. That's especially important for busy parents who may not have big empty spaces in their day.

These are some ideas that work for me and for lots of other people:

Three breaths in, three breaths out

Can you find a minute or so to sit and breathe before the kids descend on you or before you drag them out of bed? The kitchen table, the bathroom, the edge of your bed all are fine for this. Sit still and breathe in and out three times through your nostrils. Make the out-breath longer than the in-breath. This will not only have a calming effect but it will bring your mind as well as your body into the present moment.

Look out of the window

Regardless of whether what's outside is a beautiful garden or another apartment block, actually notice what's out there. What colour is the sky? Do you see people walking along the street or the road? If a car is passing by, what colour is it? This takes a couple of seconds but it unscatters the mind and brings you back into the moment with a little sense of space. In other words, you've had the space to stop and look.

Put a reminder beside the door

Once upon a time, most houses in Ireland had a tiny water font or religious image beside the door as a spiritual reminder when people left or came in. That doesn't happen anymore, but you can use the idea to get you into a mindful state. If you hang keys inside the door can you have one key on its own hook that you don't use but that reminds you to be mindful as you leave? Perhaps it could be on a key ring with a pleasant scene or a suitable quote? Or could the kids make a picture to keep beside the door as a reminder?

In the car

If you drive the children to school, could you get them to do some mindful breathing? If they are young enough, but

168

not too young, they will do it for you, at least for a while. After you've dropped the children off can you deliberately drive away mindfully, coming back again and again from those thoughts of work, school, family and so on?

I call this 'out the door mindfulness' because it can get you out the door and into the day with a minimum of stress. And the really helpful aspect of this is that mindfulness gives us a space in which to remember to be compassionate towards ourselves. When you start brooding on your faults, for instance, self-compassion can be lost as you become more stressed, so it's really helpful when mindfulness calls you back to a realisation of what you're doing.

Mindfulness can help Kevin to spot when he is ruminating and thereby increasing his own levels of stress by how he is thinking about himself or about the world. Rumination increases levels of stress by activating his Fight or Flight system with its adrenaline-fuelled readiness to deal with trouble.

When he is aware of his ruminating – on his inadequacies as a parent, for instance – he can do something about it. For one, he can give some compassion to himself instead of thinking yet another series of negative thoughts.

The more self-compassionate you are, the easier you will find it to step out of preoccupations with whether or not you are a good parent and to accept your own feelings and those of your child. In other words, the more self-compassionate you are, the more mindful you will be.

PERFECTION IS NOT REQUIRED

The many exercises in this book will help you to implement what you have read in this chapter but begin by remembering this:

- You are not setting out to be the perfect parent. Actually, a perfect parent, if such existed, would poorly equip his or her child for this imperfect world. Give compassion to yourself and to your child instead of perfection.

- It's okay to have negative emotions but they don't have to dictate to you. Allow them to come and go in their own time.

- Practise a little pause before reacting to your child – with common sense of course! If your child is about to drink a bottle of washing-up liquid, don't pause before intervening.

- Use the well-wishing practice for yourself and your child in the Self-compassion and Mindfulness Practices section on page 171.

Kevin, in our example, will find life much easier for himself and his children if he learns to accept that it's okay to be a 'good enough' parent, that nobody ever graduates with an Honours in parenting because nobody ever stops learning and that mindfulness can help him to stop harming his own happiness and that of his children by cutting out brooding and ruminating on his imperfections.

Self-compassion and Mindfulness Practices

WELL-WISHING (A VERSION FOR PARENTS)

Sit still for a few moments. Imagine that somebody has sat down in front of you, facing you. This is your child with his or her faults and virtues.

Try to generate a feeling of goodwill and well-wishing towards your child. Now say silently, 'Be happy. Be safe. Be well.' Repeat this slowly as many times as you like.

Now imagine that your child is replaced by a second person. That second person is yourself, with your faults and virtues.

Observe yourself sitting there and try to generate the same feeling of goodwill and well-wishing towards yourself that you did towards your child. And repeat the phrase 'Be happy. Be safe. Be well.' Again, repeat this as many times as you like.

If you wish, you can add the other parent (or another child or children) as characters in this practice.

If not, you can end it here. Then sit for a few moments trying to experience that sense of goodwill and well-wishing.

MINDFULNESS WITH CHILDREN

When playing with or listening to a child it's so easy to start running through your to-do list in your mind or even to sit there wishing you were doing something interesting. But childhood, as older parents could tell you, is over in a flash and it's really worth paying attention to the here and now. Giving your attention to the child you are actually with will nourish you in ways that worrying about your to-do list just won't. Here are some ways to be mindful:

- When talking to your child, look at them instead of looking at your phone. Takes an effort but it can be done!

- Listen to what your child is saying and to how he or she is saying it.

- Give answers that don't just consist of 'yes' or 'no' (though I acknowledge that the word 'No', repeated firmly, is sometimes the only antidote to pester power!).

- If your child is asleep in your arms, really try to give your full awareness to this beautiful experience.

With a teenage child it's even more important to listen with full awareness to what they are saying to you.

Teens respond much better to being listened to than to being questioned (even with the best will in the world on the parent's part). I don't mean that you never should question a teenager – sometimes it's unavoidable in their own best interest – but listening is hugely important.

GIVE 20 PER CENT

A way to stay present to a child or teenager, or to whatever, is to give about 20 per cent of your awareness to your breathing. It sounds contradictory – giving your awareness to something else in order to give your awareness to your child – but think of it as a way of keeping your awareness in the room, of not wandering away from what's going on between you.

And don't worry about getting it precisely right. It's just a matter of giving some of your awareness to your breathing. Nobody's measuring.

AFFIRMATION

'Today I am a good enough parent.'

This affirmation reminds you that perfection is not necessary, maybe not even desirable, and isn't an option anyway. But although we know this, we human beings so easily fall into the trap of judging ourselves as inadequate because we are not perfect. The affirmation helps you realise that you, as an imperfect parent, are good enough. Remember it and repeat it when you find yourself criticising yourself because you are less than perfect and, even, like everyone else on the planet, get things wrong.

REMEMBER THIS . . .

To be a 'good enough' parent, be a self-compassionate parent. Self-compassionate parents are far better able to deal with the ups and downs of guiding another person or persons through childhood than are parents who expect perfection of themselves. As well as soothing your child, soothe yourself – it makes a difference.

NOTES

- The Portuguese study was published in *Psychology and Psychotherapy* in December 2016.

'Today is my day for self-compassion.'

14

SELF-COMPASSION
AND IDENTITY

Without quite noticing it happening, Maureen has developed a 'failure' identity. When she drops her child off at pre-school in the morning before work, she feels a pang of guilt, although he himself seems happy enough to meet the day's new adventures, following an epic struggle to get dressed.

She feels another pang of guilt when she has to make sure to leave work on time to collect him. She wonders if her colleagues think less of her because of it – if they secretly feel she is putting an unfair burden of work on their shoulders.

Her husband works nights and must leave for his job before their child is ready to go to bed. She sometimes worries that her child is being unfairly deprived of parental attention and feels guilty about it. To make up for this, she spends more time playing with him than she needs to, which means he gets less sleep than if she put him to bed earlier. As a result, it's harder to get him up and out in the morning.

Maureen, so far as I can see, is one of those millions of modern heroes, male and female, who turn themselves inside out for their families in ways that previous generations could not have imagined. Yet she sees herself as failing on all fronts.

This chapter is about identity. In other words, it's about who you are or, rather, who you think you are. Your sense of who you are can change throughout the day. At one time you might be a partner, at another you might be a golfer, at another a worker, and so on. Your sense of being a failure or a success can also change according to whether something has gone well or badly for you recently. Self-compassion can help us to be friends to ourselves as we go through these varying ideas of who we are and what we're like.

WHO ARE YOU, ANYWAY?

If I were to ask you who you are, you might tell me what you do for a living, what passion drives you (music or football for instance), what your most important relationship role is (parent or partner, perhaps), your age or any one of a thousand possibilities.

For many people, all or most of the above could be true at the same time. For instance, you could be an accountant whose life revolves around your children and a passion for football. Which identity takes top place? That might depend on where you're asked the question. You could be a blogger who, to make a living, works in a shoe shop: if, say, you are being interviewed for a job writing content for a website, you would describe yourself as a blogger; among friends who have no interest in such things, or with family, you might describe yourself as working in a shoe shop, especially if it's a well-known shoe shop; and if, when you're not doing either of these things, you like to go mountain climbing, then in certain circles, you would be introduced as a mountain climber who has climbed such-and-such a mountain.

What if you were asked whether you see yourself as succeeding or failing at whatever it is you do? Then your answer would probably be influenced by whatever relevant event happened most recently. This is known in psychology as the 'recency effect'. For instance, if Alexa's branch heads the list for the most sales in the company for three weeks she might tell you she's a success. But if you come back in three weeks' time when the branch has been marooned near the bottom of the list, she might tell you she's a failure.

So who we say we are and what we think of ourselves can change not only from day to day but within the day. To add a further twist, during that time of day when energy levels are high (usually during the morning) you are more likely to feel capable of tackling whatever comes your way, and when your energy levels are low (usually around 2pm to 3pm) you may not feel up to tackling anything. You could expect to take a more upbeat view of yourself when energy is high than when you're in a slump.

From the perspective of self-compassion, it might not

matter all that much what answer you give to a hypothet-ical question as to whether you see yourself as succeeding or failing. These answers have more to do with self-esteem than with self-compassion. A fragile sense of self-esteem that is built on success, however you define it, can be splin-tered by apparent failure.

It's not so with self-compassion. Our aim in this book is to learn to be compassionate towards ourselves and to be friends with ourselves, whether or not we are successes or failures and regardless of who we are or how we describe ourselves. If Maureen can begin to see herself through the lens of self-compassion, she will quickly see that she deserves to be proud of herself and not self-critical as she pulls herself in many directions for her family while doing good work for her employer.

If she can see herself through this lens, she can see the unfairness of viewing herself as some sort of failure for not managing to become a superwoman with capabilities (such as being in two places at the one time) that do not exist in real life. As Pema Chödrön puts it in *When Things Fall Apart: Heart Advice for Difficult Times*: 'Compassion isn't some kind of self-improvement project or ideal that we're trying to live up to.'

We can make it our aim to be self-compassionate when we feel like failures as well as when we succeed; when we are parents as well as when we are salespersons; when we have let ourselves down and when we have done ourselves proud.

'We can't just jump over ourselves as if we were not there,' Pema Chödrön also said, in one of my favourite quotes. I think that's well worth looking at further. Many of our efforts at self-improvement, it seems to me, involve trying to 'jump over ourselves as if we were not there'.

Remember the concept of our common humanity (Chapter 5, page 51)? Common humanity tells us that, at this moment, millions of people are trying to 'jump over themselves as if they were not there'. They hope to land on the other side as better people.

Self-compassion enables us to approach ourselves with kindness regardless of whether or not we engage in this 'jumping over ourselves' contest and regardless of whether we succeed at it.

IF THEY KNEW . . .

Self-compassion also makes us far less scared by a thought which, in my counselling experience, is remarkably common: 'If they knew what I was really like, they wouldn't love/like me.'

It is as though we somehow think that we are hiding our 'true' identity from the world and that the world would be shocked if it could see behind the mask. We would be expelled from the herd. The news channels might even send cameras along to record the event!

Actually, as you will have gathered from the earlier part of this chapter, you don't have a single 'true' identity anyway.

You could be a blogger, a mother, a political activist and a baker all at different times and feel somewhat different in each of these roles. But that still doesn't stop us from thinking we are a fraud when our spirits are low.

With self-compassion, you know you will be a friend to yourself even though you think you know what you are 'really' like; in other words, even though you know those parts of yourself that you keep hidden from everyone else. Perhaps you are the life and soul of the party, but secretly you'd like to run away and hide. Or perhaps you're the person who hides in a corner but secretly wants to be the life and soul of the party. Whichever you are, you can see yourself through the eyes of self-compassion and can practise being a true friend to yourself.

What if you're a success as far as the world is concerned? Even then, self-compassion could be the greatest gift you can give yourself. Success is a hard act to keep up, as Alexa is finding out, and every now and then you're going to stumble and maybe even fall. If you are practising self-compassion that prospect will not be as frightening as it might otherwise seem, because, even if you do not see a brilliant success when you look in the mirror, you will still like yourself. You will know that even failure cannot take one precious thing away from you: it cannot take your own friendship towards yourself. By practising the guidelines in this book you can bring yourself to that healthy and desirable point.

This matters, especially if you base your self-worth on

being successful – and it's very difficult not to do this because our culture encourages it. The cult of celebrity means we idolise people who are seen as successful, although behind the facade they may be very troubled indeed, as we often see when that facade is ripped away.

What has celebrity culture to do with you or me, since most of us are never going to be peering out from the magazine covers in the newsagents beneath some breathless headline? Because the success culture and the celebrity culture mislead us. Under their influence, it is all too easy for those of us who are 'ordinary' people to aspire to arrive at a state of permanent success. But this state probably does not exist – certainly I have never heard of anybody to whom it could be applied.

Once again, self-compassion is the wise choice: whoever you think you are and however well or badly you think you've done, self-compassion can be the friend that accompanies you through the changing and challenging experiences of life.

And if you think yourself a failure? All the more reason to do the sometimes hard work of becoming a true friend to yourself. Maureen sees herself as a failure but she can liberate herself through learning the art of self-compassion. And liberation doesn't mean she suddenly has to start seeing herself as a success; she simply has to develop compassion for herself and watch herself blossom as a result.

So from now on, aim to make 'self-compassionate' part of your description of who you are.

Self-compassion and Mindfulness Practices

SELF-COMPASSION FOR PART OF WHO YOU ARE

What if you find it hard to be compassionate to yourself, by which I mean to your entire self? If people – family, an abusive partner or bullies, for instance – have shamed you in life or if you have become very used to seeing yourself in a very uncompassionate way, then self-compassion can feel like a tough challenge.

In that case, take a tip from Cistercian nun Sister Miriam Pollard. In her book *Acceptance: Passage into Hope*, she suggests we practise liking some part of our experience – of the world or of ourselves – that we dislike. For instance, do you find a certain person difficult? If so, you might seek just one thing about that person that you can like. Maybe the person has few redeeming features but at least she is kind to the office cat!

See if you can apply this to yourself as an exercise. Looking at those parts of yourself that you view in a negative way, can you find one aspect of yourself that's easier to be compassionate towards than others? What do you think that might be? Suppose you procrastinate, putting off challenges until they are on top of you, but perhaps this also sometimes gives you an opportunity to think about other ways of doing things. Suppose you are extremely shy but for that very reason you have developed a strong intellectual life which has given you a deep interest in the world.

Spend a little time working this out, and then see if you can look on your 'faults' with self-compassion and with a sense of friendship towards yourself. You might also try this practice, as Sister Miriam Pollard suggests, on somebody you regard as a difficult person.

STAY IN YOUR BODY

As you will have seen by now, awareness of your body is a core mindfulness practice. For this practice, keep a background awareness of your body as often as you can as you go through the day and as you go through various moods and experiences. But how? Try to connect with awareness of your posture, not by adopting a particular posture, but by becoming aware even for a few moments now and then. This is one of the most effective ways of remaining mindful throughout the day. You will drift out of awareness of your body quite often, of course, but practise bringing yourself back whenever this happens.

Try to practise awareness of your body whenever you're using your phone or whenever you're moving from one space to another, say from one room to another. Do your circumstances allow you to sit still, obviously doing nothing, during the day? If so, set aside a few minutes just to sit and be aware of your body. If you like, you can measure this with the timer on your phone.

Perhaps you are agitated or distracted at the moment because of something that's going on in your life. Even then, awareness of your body is always a possibility and is worth cultivating. The Buddha who, more than 2,000 years ago, developed the practice of mindfulness that we use today, suggested awareness of the body as a key means of cultivating mindfulness, so you'll be in good company.

AFFIRMATION

'Today is my day for self-compassion.'

Self-compassion is for every day, not just for the days when you're feeling bad or feeling good. If you use this affirmation for a day as you encounter various moods and situations, you will cultivate self-compassion for both the joys and sorrows of life. Self-compassion can enhance the joy and soften the sorrow.

REMEMBER THIS . . .

Self-compassion can make your day. Every day contains good and bad, but kindness to yourself can be a constant thread that runs through the whole day. Whatever sort of day you're having, and whether you're feeling good or bad about yourself, remember self-compassion.

'Time to take care of number one.'

15

SELF-COMPASSION AND THE
SELF-CARE ATTITUDE

Jennifer came to a workshop at the urging of a friend who reckoned she needed to practise self-care, a phrase that made Jennifer laugh. As far as she was concerned, self-care was a concept that didn't belong in the real world – at least not in her world.

At work she was a terrifically good personal assistant to a boss who saw nothing wrong with loading her with 'urgent' work late in the afternoon. Jennifer lived alone with her mother and sometimes brought the work home with her to finish after she had made dinner. The work also intruded on her weekends. Her boss also didn't bother to prepare properly for upcoming events and it was usually Jennifer who pulled the chestnuts out of the fire.

Jennifer's mother naturally liked her daughter to spend lots of time with her and was somewhat infirm, though Jennifer's sister was convinced their mother could manage a lot better than she let on.

In their mother's eyes, Jennifer's sister was the 'golden

girl' of the family and she generally left Jennifer to get on with the housework while praising Jennifer's sister who lived in the next town. Jennifer had no time for herself or for her friends. She looked tired and had become irritable. This was what had led her friend to practically drag her to a workshop.

Jennifer is a fine example of the tendency some of us have to take care of others while neglecting ourselves. Such people may reject the idea of self-care, but in fact it's the very thing they need. To be willing to give themselves that self-care, though, they may need a strong dose of self-compassion. Jennifer is also a great example of a person who has lots of compassion for others – her boss, her mother – but who doesn't direct any of that compassion towards herself. Jennifer is in danger of suffering 'compassion-fatigue', that sense of having nothing left to give and, if nothing changes, she may begin to resent all those who endlessly take from her.

But she doesn't need to resent them. She needs to adopt self-care as an attitude towards herself, to develop her self-compassion and to see that she, too, is worthy of consideration.

Let's take a look at self-care and at what we mean by it.

SELF-CARE IS AN ATTITUDE

Self-care, at least in the sense in which I'm using it in this book, isn't about showering every day and eating your porridge, however good for you these two things might be. What I mean by self-care is caring enough about yourself to take care of yourself. It's really an attitude and it can have a huge influence on your quality of life.

On the face of it, self-care can seem like a boring topic. But it isn't boring because it is so connected to how you feel about yourself. If you don't think enough of yourself to take care of yourself, then your quality of life falls far below what would otherwise be possible. Your relationships can suffer because, if you obviously don't care about yourself, other people may find it hard to care about you.

If you don't care about yourself or at least not enough to engage in self-care, you could be easy to walk all over, as in the case of Jennifer and her boss, and ultimately you could find that you become worn down by caring for other people and leaving nothing over for the person you live with 24 hours a day: yourself. In such a situation, self-compassion is crucial. People who practise self-compassion are more likely also to practise self-care and to see to it that they look after their own emotional as well as their physical needs. You will find more on this in Chapter 10 (page 121).

QUALITY OF LIFE

That's why I think it is important, in the very stressful lives we lead, to look at this issue. Why is self-care important? I mention quality of life above. Quality of life isn't something that just happens by itself. We have to make it happen by how we treat ourselves. But will you treat yourself well if you don't think you are worth caring for? If you don't care about yourself, will you give yourself a holiday if that's what you need? Or will you just decide that it's not worth it because you're not worth it? This is where self-compassion comes in. The self-compassionate approach is that you are indeed worth caring for. You don't have to have achieved anything in order to be worthy of that and you don't even have to have approved of everything you've done. No matter what, self-compassion is a gift you can give yourself. A person who believes they are worth caring for is likely to experience life very differently to a person who believes they are not.

And we are not only talking about holidays or a pleasant meal. Self-care is also about how you let yourself be treated by other people. I have seen many cases of people doing a fine job of caring for other people or their family, perhaps even for somebody with a chronic illness, who has been left to get on with it by everybody else. 'He or she is so wonderful,' everybody else says as they live their own lives, while the carer is on duty 24 hours a day, seven days a week, out of love or a sense of duty. Actually, the carer is not 'wonderful' in terms of being super-strong. Yes, he or she – usually she – often makes efforts above and beyond the ordinary, but that same person may also be exhausted and putting his or her own health at risk. To make matters worse, if and when the caring role ends, this carer may then be left empty-handed to pick up the threads of his or her life.

Human love and sacrifice are very good things and quite wonderful to see in a world that sometimes appears obsessed with gadgets and greed. Look at the efforts that people put into caring for an unwell parent or that a parent puts into caring for a child with a disability or serious illness. But self-compassion will tell them that they must leave some space, however small – some sliver of room – for themselves for the sake of their own emotional and physical wellbeing.

This doesn't only apply in the home. If you are treated badly at work, then I think you need to see that as bad for your self-care and ask yourself, or a friend you trust, what you can do about it. And self-compassion may be the very first step in allowing yourself to do that.

If you are living on your own, I think it is even more important to have a strong sense of self-compassion. Otherwise it can be too easy to let self-care slide and, in effect, to treat yourself less well than another person would treat you. Eating only microwave or takeaway meals is an example. You wouldn't (I hope) expect a guest to live on such a diet, so why expect it of yourself? (See Chapter 11, page 137, for more on compassionate eating.)

TAKING A BREAK

The tone of your day can be transformed by something as simple as taking the time to go for a coffee or just to relax, not doing anything special, just making space for yourself. Space in your day brings a sense of freedom. Recognising that freedom is a key human need will give you an incentive to find that space.

Maybe you don't make that space because it involves asking someone else to help. If you don't ask for help, other people will think you are a superwoman or superman, and you and I know that you're not – we know that you are an ordinary person like anybody else. And that you deserve your own compassion.

RECRUITING OTHERS TO HELP

Asking for help in letting others shoulder some of the burden is, for many of us, a very difficult thing to do. Back in the days before navigational aids some of us were willing to drive around in circles before asking for directions. Others put in long hours at their desk after nightfall because they are reluctant (it may not even occur to them) to ask their boss to consider doing things differently.

Suppose your sister has phoned you every day for over a year to recite a list of complaints about her ex-husband's past behaviour. It goes on for an hour and it's always the same list. Suppose also that your sister shows little interest in your life when you try to get a word in and quickly steers the conversation back to her favourite topic. If you lack self-compassion and if you say to yourself, 'Well, she needs to let off steam and I don't have anything very interesting to say anyway', then it becomes very easy for her to disrespect your time. If you actively practise compassion towards yourself, you may be more inclined to say something like: 'Look, I love talking to you and it sounds like X was a cad, but let's talk about what's happening in your day now and I'd like to talk about what happens in my day too.' That is self-care in practice.

CARING TOO MUCH AND RUNNING ON EMPTY

The world needs helpful people – they make such an enormous difference to so many people's lives. But if you leave nothing for yourself, then you can end up feeling put-upon and irritable. You could even end up resenting other people, maybe ultimately sinking into depression and despair. Jennifer's friend could see that Jennifer was part of the way down this road. She was becoming increasingly tired and snappy, not because she had ceased caring but because she cared too much. As far as her friend was concerned, the fact that her boss regularly described her as a 'lifesaver' was less important than Jennifer's need to care for her own life.

Those who are natural carers have to recognise that they don't have endless reserves of everything to give, otherwise they will one day find themselves running on empty. That means they have to look out for themselves as well as for others. Doing so is an expression of self-compassion.

And remember that getting more freedom and space doesn't have to mean getting on a bicycle and cycling around the world. Freedom could mean simply allowing yourself to walk around the block or to go into town and wander around the shops buying more or less nothing and coming back home when you feel like it. This freedom can mean that sometimes you get to choose the movie that you and your partner will go to. Maybe it means being able to sit in a room on your own, shut the door and read, do a crossword puzzle, play solitaire or whatever else it is that you want to do.

If you're self-compassionate and if you believe in self-care, you will carve out those little areas of freedom.

I've said that freedom is a basic human need and so is play or fun. Again, bringing playfulness into your life is an important aspect of self-care. A proverb says 'All work and no play makes Jack a dull boy.' The same applies to Jill. No play can make for a very unhappy boy or girl who feels very put-upon and whose quality of life is poor. Again, with self-compassion you can build a more playful life because fun really matters and is a genetic need. For some people, play is going to a movie; for others, it's having a laugh with a friend; for others, it's kicking a ball around; for others, it's gardening – there are so many possibilities. Some psychologists see the playfulness of young children and young animals as a genetically driven form of learning. Play gets translated into fun later on in life.

So in practising self-care you're practising a philosophy

of life for yourself and you are meeting basic, fundamental, human needs. Your greatest aid in ensuring that you will put this philosophy into practice is self-compassion.

Self-compassion and Mindfulness Practices

NOTING SELF-COMPASSION

Think of examples in the last 24 hours of kindness towards yourself:

- Did you catch yourself speaking harshly to yourself and correct it?

- Did you carry out a task earlier than usual so that you won't be rushing when it's due?

- Did you take the time to have a pleasant meal instead of rushing through any old thing?

- Did you make time for a mindfulness practice or a self-compassion practice in your day?

Get into the habit of making a mental note like this every day. This could be at any time during the day or before you go to bed at night. Choose whatever works for you. A practice like this will remind you to be self-compassionate and will make a real difference over time.

You may not be familiar with the practice of reviewing your day like this while you are still in the middle of it. But if you do it, the practice can open your eyes to how you treat yourself and to changes you could make. The changes may be small at first (giving yourself time for a relaxing stroll at lunchtime, for instance), but they can add up to a huge difference in your quality of life.

JUST RESTING

For a few minutes, sit in relaxation without making any demands of any kind on yourself.

Allow yourself to rest in the same way that somebody who has just finished some hard physical work allows themselves to rest. Let yourself sink into the chair, perhaps with a long out-breath when you sit down.

While you are doing this, whenever you notice that your mind has begun to solve problems, just use the phrase 'not happening now' and bring your awareness back to resting. This is both a mindfulness practice and an act of self-kindness.

AFFIRMATION

'Time to take care of number one.'

'Taking care of number one' is sometimes used in a critical way to describe someone who puts themselves first unfairly at the expense of other people. But remember that 'taking care of number one' in the ways described in this chapter is not only okay to do but actually necessary. And this affirmation can prompt you to ask, 'When did I last give time to taking care of number one and when's the next time I can do it?'

REMEMBER THIS . . .

Self-care is fuelled by self-compassion. It isn't just a concept – it's a behaviour; something you actually do. How can you do it today?

'I celebrate
my liberation
from . . .'

16

SELF-COMPASSION AND
RECOVERY

Emma sees herself as weak when it comes to drink. After work she will generally go to the pub with her friend and it is their habit to order a bottle of white wine and two glasses and to sit and drink while talking about the latest dramas at work. Sometimes Emma manages to go home after that, but sometimes the drinking goes on. She likes to read but she just falls asleep nowadays whenever she tries to read a book after going home. And the same applies to watching movies on the television. She doesn't like having hangovers in the morning but she sees herself as way too weak to go through all of the unpleasantness of giving up drinking. At least when she is drinking she feels like a person who is fun and strong and sociable

Emma has tried giving up a few times but she found it a challenge and she hated herself when she failed.

GIVING UP IS HARD TO DO

Giving up any behaviour on which we are dependent is not an easy thing and there's no point in pretending it is. But perhaps you can see how much easier it would be for Emma to make that choice and to go through the pain of giving up drinking if she thought well of herself. After all, if you think that you are weak and somehow inferior, and if drinking makes you feel better, then your belief is a contributor to the pull towards engaging in that behaviour.

In this case drink, or other drugs, can be like a magnetic, always-available option. Emma needs to take that option away but she also needs to comfort and soothe herself as she goes through the travails of giving up. Self-compassion is hugely beneficial in doing this and will make her far more unwilling to behave towards herself in such a damaging way.

Giving up needs to be a self-compassionate act. Indeed, it can be so difficult that sometimes I think it needs to be a selfish act in order for it to really work. It needs to be self-compassionate because the harder we are on ourselves the more likely we are to reach for some sort of relief and, unfortunately, that relief may come from whatever it is that we are dependent on. It needs to be selfish, if the dependence is very strong, because the stronger the dependence the longer the road to recovery. However, recovery usually benefits the people around you so it is not entirely selfish.

But self-compassion is the key, not only in encouraging you to work yourself free of dependence but of surviving relapse. I mentioned in Chapter 9 (page 107) that people who are self-compassionate are more successful when they try to change their habits in a more healthy direction. That's partly because, if you are harsh on yourself for breaking a diet, you may, to escape the pain of that harshness, turn to the comfort of eating. So relapse creates a need to escape self-criticism which, in turn, creates a further relapse. And so you become caught in a vicious circle.

Exactly the same process applies if it's a case of trying to give up and cut down on drinking, smoking or other drugs or behaviours. But self-compassion, by replacing harsh criticism with an attitude of kindness, aids the return to recovery.

The recovery road is long and you need to be a friend to yourself to get along it successfully.

PLEASURE AND THE CRAVING SYSTEM

One specific point I want to make is that if you have given up a behaviour or substance some time ago but you still crave it, this is not a sign of weakness on your part. The 'craving system' in the brain seems to operate independently of logic and independently of what you might call the 'thinking system'. Long after you've decided that the behaviour or substance is bad for you, the craving system can still want it. Indeed, long after you've stopped getting any substantial amount of pleasure from it, the craving system still wants it.

Why would you stop getting any substantial amount of pleasure from it and why, in that case, would you still want it? First, the brain tends to moderate the amount of pleasure you get from the substance or activity to bring it back down to a normal level, to restore a state of balance. That's why you'll enjoy the first square of chocolate more than the tenth – gradually the 'hit' from the chocolate has been turned down. I really wish we didn't have this design feature, but we do. This is also why, after you've had one or two drinks, you may not get very much additional pleasure from drinking more, though the craving system still wants it. Similarly, if you're a smoker you may have noticed that after you've had the first cigarette of the day, the rest of the cigarettes in the pack don't bring you much more than a foul taste in your mouth, but the craving system still wants another smoke.

The primitive craving system operates independently of our thinking and even of our pleasure systems. It remembers you can get pleasure from alcohol, cigarettes, cocaine and so on, and it wants you to keep trying. That's how all our brains are designed – yours and everyone else's.

For that reason it is quite unnecessary and unhelpful to condemn yourself for the fact that you're still craving something long after you gave it up. Instead, you need to thank yourself for having made this decision in your life and you need to allow the craving to pass in its own time. Cravings usually pass reasonably quickly unless you keep them alive by focusing on them. Yes, they return, but each time they come back, allow them to pass again. Eventually cravings largely die away – but you have to give them time to do so.

When giving up something that you know is bad for you I think it is important also that you do not do it in any sort of punishing way. Really, in order to successfully drop a behaviour (and in the word behaviour I am including substance abuse), you need to find something else that you can do instead, something satisfying or pleasurable. If you decide to cut down on drinking, then sitting and staring at the four walls really is not a viable alternative.

SWITCHING THE FOCUS FROM ABSTINENCE TO ENJOYMENT

This is where self-compassion comes in because, if you take a self-compassionate approach to yourself, you will be willing to seek out these more pleasurable and more self-satisfying activities. For example, if you give up drinking you could allow yourself to spend extra time at the theatre or cinema or, if you like reading, you could spend some time reading which you definitely wouldn't have been able to do to any effect when you were drinking. You could also arrange to meet friends who are not completely involved in drinking. You could enjoy the weekends more and take a pleasant walk, say, on a Saturday or Sunday morning that you might otherwise not have taken.

Remember to switch the focus from the absence of whatever it is you're craving to whatever it is you're enjoying. If you are on holiday and not drinking but lots of people around you are throwing back the beer and wine, it is very easy to tell yourself that you can't possibly enjoy your holiday because you're not drinking. They, you tell yourself, are all enjoying themselves so very much more than you are.

As a matter of fact, if drinking is just normal for them they are not really getting any extra enjoyment out of it – it's just something they do every day anyway. What you need to focus on here is not how much other people are enjoying themselves because they are drinking, but how much you yourself are enjoying this meal, these sights, this conversation, this activity. In order to do that successfully you need to have activities and conversations going on that are appealing to you and that you will enjoy.

SPOTTING – AND QUASHING – EUPHORIC RECALL

Mindfulness also helps you to spot when you're fooling yourself. You are most likely to fool yourself through a process called 'euphoric recall'. Euphoria is a state in which we have a heightened sense of pleasure. Euphoric recall, then, is remembering a heightened state of pleasure and it's a pitfall for people trying to drop drinking, taking drugs or engaging in behaviours on which they are dependent. For instance, when I stopped drinking for an experimental year (which has turned into four years so far) I found myself, when walking by a certain pub, imagining how much fun it would be to sit inside the pub, drinking. It was as though I had a memory of wonderful, warm, cheery times at the bar. Yet when I stepped back mentally from what was going on, I was able to remind myself that I had found this pub a rather dark, smelly, depressing place which I had avoided. Fun? You're kidding me, I told my craving brain.

Being able to take this kind of view is also really helpful when you're trying to give up other behaviours. And the practice of mindfulness will make it easier and easier for you to see through the illusion of euphoric recall, which is really just a trick played by the craving system.

Who do you want to be anyway? Do you want to be a person who can read late at night? Do you want to be a physically fitter person? Cultivate an idea of what and who you want to be, make it a positive and achievable one, realise that you deserve to get yourself to that point and it will make it much, much easier to go through what you have to go through to get there. We live in an age in which people develop dependencies on all sorts of things. We know that many people are seriously dependent on prescription drugs. People also become dependent on gambling, video-gaming, pornography, and on various other things. There is no end to the range of dependencies that can afflict us. I have come across people who are dependent on knitting.

To me, one of the key things about dependencies is that they make us unhappy and, if we're going to be compassionate towards ourselves, then we will almost certainly want to do something about that. Self-compassion can help greatly with that project.

Self-compassion and Mindfulness Practices

URGE SURFING

One of cravings' little tricks is to tell you that you will feel it always and that it is never going to go away until you give in. In fact, cravings fade very quickly. Yes, they come back again (and giving in won't stop that from happening) but they will fade very quickly again if you allow them to. To help convince your brain of this fact, try a little 'urge surfing' now and then. Here's how it works:

- Sit still for two minutes and don't change your posture at all during that time: no shuffling, shifting, squirming or scratching. Try to feel compassion for yourself as you do this.

- Now wait for a desire to shuffle, shift, squirm or scratch to arise. Whether what you feel is an itch or a desire to move, observe compassionately what it feels like but without acting on it. For instance, if it's an itch where is it? Is it in a different place now from where it was a few moments ago? Is it more or less intense than a few moments ago? Does its intensity change as you breathe in and out? When the two minutes are up you can shift and scratch all you want.

The purpose of this exercise is to demonstrate to you that cravings arise and fall. No craving stays put for ever: it comes and goes. This is helpful to know when you are trying to drop your dependence on a substance or a behaviour. And remember, the return of a craving isn't a sign of weakness – it's a sign of being human.

MINDFUL BREATHING: THE CALMING OUT-BREATH

The out-breath is calming and you may have noticed that rest after exertion is often signalled by a long out-breath as our chest muscles relax. Most of the time we tend to ignore the out-breath but we gain a lot by seeing it as a resource for mindful relaxation. To work with the out-breath, put aside a few minutes in which you will observe the in-breath and out-breath, gradually allowing the out-breath to become longer than the in-breath.

- You could start by counting to five, reasonably slowly, as your in-breath takes place. Now observe your out-breath (you don't have to make it happen), also counting slowly.

- Now allow your out-breath to become longer than your in-breath as you breathe in and out by two beats, e.g. count to five as you take an in-breath and to seven as you take an out-breath. If a longer or shorter count (7–9 or 4–6 for instance) works better for you, then use that.

Remember, as always, to keep returning your attention to your breathing and counting every time your mind wanders off.

'I celebrate my liberation from . . .'

Because dropping a dependency is challenging, it's terribly easy to lose sight of the benefits of succeeding. If that happens we may focus on the pain of the challenge and not on the gain – and that makes it even harder to succeed. Telling yourself that you celebrate your liberation shines a positive light on the whole effort. Over time, reminding yourself that, 'I celebrate my liberation from drinking/smoking or whatever it may be' will lighten the load and shorten the path.

And don't wait until after you've successfully given something up before you start allowing yourself to say good things about yourself. Remember that as a self-compassionate person you are trying to be a good friend to the person you already are. As a good friend you can advise yourself on how to deal with this dependence and you can help yourself through the whole process of recovery.

REMEMBER THIS . . .

The road to recovery is paved with self-compassion. Other people can help enormously – but the first person whose friendship you need to be able to count on is the person in the mirror.

‘Wishing you well.’

17

PAST, PRESENT
AND FUTURE

Abigail is in her mid-fifties and, whether she looks back or looks forward, the picture is rather glum. When she looks back she can see the ambitions that she used to have as a teenager, how she became diverted into other pathways, such as the necessity of working at a job she could get when she needed the money, rather than her dream job. Looking back from now, with the benefit of hindsight, she can see different paths she could have taken if she had known about them at the time.

She thinks she ought to have known about them because these paths seem so obvious from where she is now. Although the job she has is quite satisfactory and is one that many people would be very pleased to have, Abigail nonetheless sees herself as having failed, so to speak, in the past. And that judgement makes it difficult for her to fully enjoy her achievements in the present.

When she looks to the future the picture is also glum. She buys into the most negative media reports of what it is like to grow older and assumes that this will be her fate. She already sees herself as having almost no autonomy, no influence over how the future will be and, if you like, she already sees herself as failing herself for the rest of her life.

Abigail is completely neglecting to give herself any credit for the fact that life is not thoroughly and completely pre-planned. In life we have a general idea of the direction we want to take but – as might happen if you were walking through a forest – the path unfolds before us and sometimes takes us to places in which we didn't expect to find ourselves. So Abigail's rigid view of how her life should have worked out is at odds with how life really is. Similarly she is already pre-judging her future in the gloomiest way.

If Abigail could be compassionate towards her past, present and future self she could begin to enjoy a sense of acceptance that she has never had. It just so happens that Abigail makes a point of buying a lottery ticket every week and dreams of what she would do if she became a multi-millionaire. But for Abigail, self-compassion could bring more happiness than winning the lottery.

KINDFULNESS FOR LIFE

In practising kindfulness – mindful self-compassion – we usually seek to cultivate the ability to be a true friend to ourselves in any given moment. But what about our future and past selves? It's all very well to say that the past is gone and the future is not yet here, but it is a characteristic of human beings that thoughts of the past and of the future weigh heavily on us. That we can conjure up images of the past – of people, places and activities – as if on a cinema screen in the mind, as well as images of the future, may make us unique in the animal world.

It also means we can suffer emotionally about past and future events even though they exist only in the mind. We can declare all we like that 'the past is gone and the future is not yet come' but if you pranged your car off a truck yesterday and you're getting the repair bill for the truck tomorrow, you are unlikely to find that declaration comforting. That's why I think it's really important to be able to extend compassion to our past and future selves.

CHOICES YES, BUT CONDITIONS TOO

In relation to both, it helps to bear in mind that we don't have a free hand in how our lives turn out. As with Abigail's story at the start of this chapter, our lives are shaped not only by choices but also by conditions and demands.

If you pick any point in your life, conditions led you there. Three babies born today in the Sahara Desert, in Manhattan and in Papua New Guinea will be shaped by very different conditions as well as by the choices they later make. These conditions include their upbringing, their economic and social class, their own personality make-up, and events happening in their environment.

At each point in your life – and I'm drawing here both from Buddhist and Western psychology – you made a choice. Sometimes you knew you were making a choice and sometimes it happened so quickly it felt automatic – an analogy might be following links on the Internet: each click is a choice that might take less than a second to make but it's still a choice.

That choice then became another condition in your life. For instance, making a choice to continue to live with your parents creates a very different pathway in your life from making a choice to leave and live on your own.

But not all sets of choices are equal. For instance, if you have no money and no job, then leaving home could be a very challenging choice. If you have money and great career prospects, leaving home could be a really easy choice. Similarly, if you're scared of the big bad world, leaving home could feel quite difficult, whereas if you are a very confident person leaving home could, again, feel easy.

So that's one of the insights that helps you to bring self-compassion to your past and future: you are not in control of all the conditions that shape your life; and while you've made thousands of choices and will continue to do so, your choices can be limited by these conditions and by your own personality.

GOOD LUCK, BAD LUCK AND THE UNKNOWN

Choices are also influenced by factors we're unaware of at the time. For instance, as Dr John Bargh of Yale University has pointed out (in *Before You Know It: The Unconscious Reasons We Do What We Do*), if you go shopping when you're sad, you're likely to buy more stuff and to be willing to spend more for it. So if the store plays romantic heart-break songs it's setting you up to hand over your cash, or your card, more often. It hasn't hypnotised you, but it has nudged you in that direction.

The effect of your choices is also limited by good luck and bad luck. Sometimes, especially in looking back at choices that did not work out well, it's better to ask if it seemed like the right choice at the time than to berate yourself for how it worked out. Suppose you are offered a better job at a higher salary in another city. You weigh up the pros and cons and, having done so, you move to the new city. On your first day at work, the company announces it is unable to meet its debts and is closing down. Your replacement at the old company started that morning and you cannot get your job back.

In the future looking back you may ruminate on what a rotten decision you made. Actually, you didn't make a rotten decision. Almost anyone, weighing up the factors that were known to you – more money, better prospects, bright lights – would have made the same decision. The outcome was bad, yes, because an unknown factor came crashing in and upended everything. To lament that outcome is fine but to criticise yourself for having made a bad decision is not – because the decision, based on what you knew, was good in itself.

Everything I have said about your past journey applies to your future journey: your choices will be influenced, not only by what you want, but by unpredictable conditions (a collapse/boom in the economy for instance) and sometimes by conditions outside your awareness (that sad music in the supermarket).

It makes sense, then, to bring self-compassion to the person you were in the past and the person you will be in the future. This isn't to say that you approve of every single thing that you have done or will do: it recognises that you are a human being who sometimes makes choices that work out well and sometimes makes choices that work out badly in conditions that are not all under his or her control.

YOU ARE NOT A PROJECT

Back to that point about you as a human being: in the West, at any rate, we seem to have fallen into the trap of looking on life as a project. So we try to learn how to put together a successful life as a partner, employee, meditator and so on. We judge ourselves as though we ought to be able to wrap up that project really neatly – as if it was all as simple as baking a cake – so that if somebody were to examine our record they would give us the top grade.

But here's the thing: you are not a project; you're a human being and, like all human beings, you are sometimes good, sometimes bad; sometimes great, sometimes awful; sometimes a success, sometimes a failure. That's not necessarily an easy place to be – the bright and shiny objects of your life mixed in with the junk – and, again, that is why we need to give ourselves self-compassion and to be a friend to ourselves.

Similarly, you are not an investment. You are a human being and all of the messy things described in this book happen to you. We talk about 'investing' in people, in the young for instance. In some countries, we load students with heavy debts by the time they finish college, as part of our 'investment' in them. So the investment myth is a strong force in our culture. Again, from the perspective of self-compassion, you need to challenge that view of yourself whenever you find it has crept into your attitude. A robot is an investment; a human being is not.

Many people are scared of the future because they fear they will be badly treated again and will fall flat on their faces yet again. Well, yes, you will from time to time be badly treated and you will from time to time fall flat on your face. Why not replace some of your fear with a commitment to be compassionate to yourself and a true friend to yourself when these things happen?

In short, self-compassion is not just for now: it's for life.

Self-compassion and Mindfulness Practices

THREE IMAGES

Imagine that you are looking at three images. One depicts yourself in the past; another you as you are now; and a third is an image of you in the future. For the first two, you could use actual images but it may be more convenient simply to imagine them.

Looking at the image of yourself in the present, wish yourself well in the ways we've already done in previous practices: 'Be happy. Be safe. Be well.'

Now look at the image of yourself in the past, and again wish yourself well: 'Be happy. Be safe. Be well.'

Finally, look at the image of yourself in the future and wish yourself well: 'Be happy. Be safe. Be well.'

If you like, you can now imagine all three images together and again wish yourself well: 'Be happy. Be safe. Be well.'

In doing this exercise you set aside, for now, the feelings you may have about past events and future expectations and instead you generate self-compassion. This exercise can do a great deal to break the chain of rumination about events that are now outside of your control.

BREATHING IN THE PAST AND FUTURE

This is a variation on the old Buddhist practice known as 'tonglen' that I described more fully in Chapter 5 (page 56).

As you breathe in, think of your own past – not necessarily in detail, but just try to have a general sense of it. Imagine that you are compassionately and with acceptance breathing in that past and that you are breathing out compassion to yourself in that past. Do this for a few in-breaths and out-breaths.

Now turn to your future. Imagine that you are breathing in the future, of yourself and of the world, and breathing out compassion to yourself and to the world. Do this for a few in-breaths and out-breaths.

The purpose of this exercise is to create an acceptance of your past and future selves so as to enhance your experience of your present moment.

AFFIRMATION

'Wishing you well.'

Use this affirmation to wish your future and past selves well. Wishing ourselves well can bring about an important change in our relationship with our past and future by replacing at least some of our regret, anger and anxiety with kindness and compassion.

REMEMBER THIS . . .

Self-compassion: it's for life. Not only can we bring the practice of self-compassion with us through life, but we can also look compassionately on ourselves in the past and future. In my experience, this can greatly enhance how we feel about ourselves in the present.

CONCLUSION: A FUTURE OF SELF-COMPASSION

Suppose you are walking through a forest and in its depths you meet a mysterious figure who hands you a bag of gold and vanishes. You bring the gold home and the next day you go off to have it tested. You find that it is, indeed, gold and that you are now a very rich person. Armed with this knowledge, you might decide to splash out in ways you've always wanted to do or you might decide to carefully invest your gold and to try to have a continuous income, or you might do something halfway in between. What you probably wouldn't do is take your bag of gold, empty it into a nearby river and allow the current to carry it away.

THE TRUE GOLD

Learning to be compassionate towards yourself is that bag of gold. It is probably worth a great deal more than real gold – if you had a lot of money but you lacked self-compassion you would not really be better off than a person who had little money and who also lacked self-compassion. Self-compassion, in my view, is the real gold in life.

And that is why I think it is so important that you continue to make it part of your life and that you continue to use the practices in this book. It may be that you will only find one or two that stick in your mind but, as with a good recipe book, if one or two click with you, and if you use them, then you've got your money's worth. That's because each time you use the practice you will re-awaken the experience of reading the book and you will re-awaken self-compassion as a force within yourself.

USING THE BOOK

So, experiment – find out what works best for you here and make a point of using it. Perhaps every now and then you might take the book out, open it at a random page and read. Perhaps you might highlight sections in the book to read in the future. These are all ways to help you to maintain your self-compassion and to keep that sack of gold in your possession to help you into the future. And just as those who know you would hopefully benefit from your having lots and lots of gold – at least they would hope so! – so will those around you and those dearest to you benefit greatly from your practice of self-compassion. It will make you a different, warmer person to be around.

To cultivate self-compassion into the future, remember that this practice has three important components:

1. Kindness towards the person you already are.

2. Awareness of our common humanity.

3. Mindfulness.

COMPASSION FIRST

The good news for all of us is that our practice of mindful self-compassion – kindfulness – doesn't end here. It's a practice for life and deciding to make it a practice for life is a true act of self-friendship. After all, as explained in Chapter 17 (page 213), the path before you will sometimes take you where you want to go and sometimes where you don't want to go; so, 'Compassion first'!

Remembering those three components listed above will help you to deepen and explore the process of being a true friend to yourself and what a great gift that is to give yourself.

The internal critic will still pipe up from time to time, declaring that self-compassion is a cop-out and that, really, you should be giving yourself some character-building grief.

When that happens, remind yourself of the many benefits of self-compassion, for instance that self-compassionate people are good in relationships and are good at moving forward in their lives because they have lost the fear of harsh and extreme self-criticism. Instead they have taken on the perspective of a true friend who cares about them and, by extension, cares about those who are close to them and who are good for them.

One of my favourites among the practices in the course is to ask myself 'What would a friend say?' when faced with a dilemma. I think this is so helpful because a friend on the one hand won't be afraid to speak the truth and on the other hand always does so from the perspective of caring for you.

KEEPING SELF-COMPASSION IN MIND

To continue to practise self-compassion, it's really important not to forget about it in the busyness of your life. A critical email, a cutting remark, or even just a crowded to-do list, can all push self-compassion to one side. So figuring out a way to remember to be self-compassionate will be really helpful in keeping this practice in your life from now on.

One way to do this, is to choose an affirmation from the book or, indeed, a favourite affirmation of your own. Get into the habit of saying it to yourself as you are getting up every morning and before you move forward into the day.

That, in itself, will help to remind you to take the self-compassionate path. All the better if you can remember to repeat the affirmation during the day (perhaps at lunch-time) and each evening (perhaps when you leave work).

I like the affirmation, 'Compassion first' because it

suggests an approach I can include when dealing with any situation. That is especially so when I might be under a pressure of time, feeling anxious or having to deal with a mistake I've made. 'Compassion first' as an affirmation adds a helpful and friendly ingredient to the mix of thoughts in my mind at such times.

I like to practise mindfulness by becoming aware of my breathing in my nose. I find it's a good and really simple way to bring my thoughts and awareness back from wherever they've wandered off to. And I also try to remind myself frequently that acceptance is a core aspect of mindfulness.

It's important to work out what your preferred mindfulness practice is and to find a way to bring that into your day, even if you can only manage a very, very short practice.

Do you remember 'bombu nature' (Chapter 9, page 107)? It means we are never going to do anything perfectly and that includes self-compassion! Accepting that fact and that aspect of our nature is, in my opinion, really beneficial in how I approach my life. It reminds me that there isn't some perfect person I would be if I wasn't who I am – I would still have that bombu nature and perfection would not be an option.

Thank you for taking the journey with me in this book. I hope and believe you will find it a worthwhile journey all the way through your life.

I leave you with this seven-day course in self-compassion,

one you can take now or at any time in the future. Do it whatever way you want to do it: all seven days in a row, spread out over weeks or even months, in a different order from the one I give here . . . any way you like.

Do it, in other words, in the spirit of self-compassion.

SEVEN DAYS TO SELF-COMPASSION

DAY ONE: LIKING WHO YOU ARE

Begin by promising to like who you are right now. Even if you don't feel it, you can still promise. You don't have to like all of your behaviours, but you can like the person behind the behaviours. That is the person who needs your support and compassion, regardless of whether you want to change aspects of your life.

Practice: Well-wishing practice (Chapter 6, page 76). Call to mind someone you like, love or admire. Wish them well. You could use the phrase 'Be happy. Be safe. Be well.' Now replace that person with yourself as you are – no need to be perfect, just you as you are. Now wish yourself well: 'Be happy. Be safe. Be well.'

Affirmation: Use this a few times during the day: 'Today I befriend the person I already am.' It's really good to use this first thing in the morning.

229

DAY TWO: COMPASSION FOR YOUR BODY

Your body, like everyone else's, is the subject of magazine articles, books, public-health campaigns, advertising . . . the list goes on. Poor body — imagine being endlessly judged like that! Give your body some compassion by doing a mindful body scan (mindfulness of the body as a practice goes back thousands of years).

Practice: Body scan with compassion (Chapter 2, page 24). Bring your awareness to the top of your head and move it slowly down your body to your feet. Do so with compassion for your body regardless of whether you approve of your body or not.

Affirmation: 'Kindfulness is always in my power.'

DAY THREE: SELF-COMPASSIONATE EATING

How and what we eat tells us a lot about our self-compassion or the absence of it. Today choose to eat in a way that expresses self-compassion. Cooking something pleasant, sitting down to eat, making time to eat in a relaxed way, all give the message to yourself that you are a valued guest in your own life.

Practice: Mindful eating (Chapter 11, page 137). For at least part of a meal, better still a whole meal, give attention to your eating, to taste and texture for instance. See how this enhances the experience.

Affirmation: 'Today is my day for self-compassion.'

DAY FOUR: LET FEELINGS PASS

A key mindfulness approach is to allow feelings to pass in their own time without trying to get rid of them. For instance, if find you're in a negative mood, then instead of talking endlessly to yourself about it, you can allow it to pass while you get on with whatever you need to do. This is far more helpful than brooding on negativity.

Practice: Mindful breathing (Chapter 1, page 10). Notice the sensation of breathing in your nostrils. When your mind wanders to different thoughts, silently say 'thinking' and return to observing your breathing. Do this for a few minutes a few times during the day.

Affirmation: 'This moment, a moment of kindfulness.'

DAY FIVE: CONNECT TO THE GOOD FRIEND

Each of us has, in our mind, a harsh critic who attacks us over everything, from how we live our life to forgetting to buy milk in the shop. In practising self-compassion we try to listen to the good friend in our minds, not the harsh critic. The good friend can encourage and comfort us and can put us right in a supportive way.

Practice: Noting self-compassion (Chapter 15, page 197). A couple of times today, perhaps at lunchtime and bedtime, recall when you have been self-compassionate and when you have been harsh to yourself. Pledge to increase the self-compassion and to reduce the harshness.

Affirmation: 'Time to take care of number one.' Yes, you can take care of your own needs too . . .

DAY SIX: BOMBU NATURE

This Buddhist concept refers to the fact that we are imperfect beings who need not demand perfection from ourselves – such a demand is bound to fail! When you stumble, when you forget, when you say something silly – it's bombu nature and it's okay to be that imperfect being.

Practice: Spotting bombu nature (Chapter 9, page 116). Spot small examples today of bombu nature in yourself and others. Remind yourself that they simply arise from being human and that, usually, criticism is not called for.

Affirmation: 'Compassion first.' A great affirmation to use when facing imperfections.

DAY SEVEN: COMPASSION FOR PAST, PRESENT AND FUTURE SELF

We can acknowledge past failings and suffering in a compassionate way just as we try to give compassion to ourselves in the present. We can also, now, face our future with compassion for ourselves in whatever it will bring. This can help to reduce brooding on the past or anxiety about the future.

Practice: Giving compassion as you are now (Chapter 7, page 88). Think of people who were important to you in the past, perhaps people who shaped your life in some way or who had expectations of you. Addressing them silently as you are now (not as you think they wanted you to be), wish them well: 'Be happy. Be safe. Be well.'

Affirmation: 'Today I am good enough.' Give yourself the gift of this affirmation as often as you need it today.

INDEX

and anxiety 40–41

being a friend to who you
are 4–5, 7, 9, 11–12, 63,
65–6, 77, 203, 214–15, 219,
225 see also acceptance
Tend and Befriend culti-
vation 123, 124–5, 129,
134

benefits of 39–48

in challenging circum-
stances 72–4

continuing the practice of
223–8

and depression 40–41

in eating 139–45, 193,
230–31

and eating disorders 74–5

fostering change 63–5

freedom through 6–7

freedom to choose 145

and healthy behaviours 45

and identity see identity

as an inside job 3

and listening 67, 75,
149–50, 151–2 see also
listening

lost when comparing
ourselves to others
94–7

mindfulness with see
mindful self-compassion
('kindfulness')

and motivation 43–4

noting 197–8, 232

and our common
humanity 51–9 see also
humanity, common

and our flaws and imper-
fections see imperfections

and parenting see parenting

and recovery from depend-
ency see dependency,
self-compassionate
recovery from

and relationships see relationships

sacred cows and the denial
of see sacred cows/
conditions of worth

and self-care see self-care

seven day course in 229–33

sharing in the happiness of
others (mudita) 93–103

self-criticism 5–6, 20, 57,
107–8, 231–2

asking who is talking 67

and assumptions about
others 147–8, 150

yellow
kite

books to help you live a good life

Join the conversation and tell
us how you live a #goodlife

🐦 @yellowkitebooks
📘 YellowKiteBooks
📌 Yellow Kite Books
📷 YellowKiteBooks

For more on self-compassion,
including free audios and tips, go to:

www.padraigomorain.com/kindfulness

You may enjoy reading Padraig O'Morain's other books:

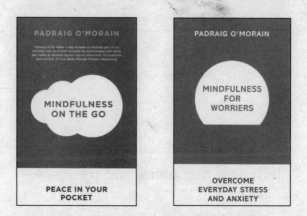

You may enjoy these books that cover similar topics, also published by Yellow Kite:

Self-Compassion by **Kristin Neff**
(ISBN 978-1444738179)

The Power of Now by **Eckhart Tolle**
(ISBN 978-0340733509)

The Gift of Silence by **Kankyo Tannier**
(ISBN 978-1473673434)